Ralph Payne-Gallwey

Letters to Young Shooters

(First Series) on the Choice and use of a Gun

Ralph Payne-Gallwey

Letters to Young Shooters
(First Series) on the Choice and use of a Gun

ISBN/EAN: 9783744720984

Printed in Europe, USA, Canada, Australia, Japan

Cover: Foto ©Andreas Hilbeck / pixelio.de

More available books at **www.hansebooks.com**

LETTERS

TO

YOUNG SHOOTERS

(FIRST SERIES)

ON THE CHOICE AND USE OF A GUN

BY

SIR RALPH PAYNE-GALLWEY BART.

SECOND EDITION

LONDON
LONGMANS, GREEN, AND CO.
AND NEW YORK: 15 EAST 16th STREET
1892

All rights reserved

MY DEAR WALSINGHAM,

As your skill with the gun is unsurpassed; and as your knowledge of Game and Wildfowl—in regard to their natural history, and their management in the field, so as to afford true sport—is, I consider, unrivalled, I therefore dedicate this book to you. I shall feel very satisfied if all young sportsmen who peruse it will endeavour to follow in your footsteps—even at a distance.

Believe me,
Your affectionate Cousin,
RALPH PAYNE-GALLWEY.

CONTENTS

LETTER		PAGE
I.	REMARKS ON GUNS OLD AND NEW . . .	1-7
II.	ON THE QUALITY, MANUFACTURE, AND COST OF MODERN GUNS	8-22
III.	HAMMER, HAMMERLESS, AND EJECTOR GUNS . .	23-33
IV.	ON THE FIT AND CHOICE OF A GUN, AND THE BEST GUN TO USE AS ADAPTED TO DIFFERENT SHOOTERS	34-53
V.	THE CHOICE OF GUNS (*continued*), WITH REMARKS ON THEIR FASTENINGS, THE MERITS OF STEEL AND DAMASCUS, AND THE LENGTH OF GUN-BARRELS	54-66
VI.	THE MERITS OF CHOKES AND CYLINDERS, AS APPLIED TO THEIR EFFECT ON GAME AND SUITABILITY TO THE SHOOTER . . .	67-77
VII.	THE MERITS OF CHOKES AND CYLINDERS (*continued*)	78-90
VIII.	HOW TO SHOOT SAFELY, WITH REMARKS ON LOADERS, AND THE SAFE HANDLING OF A GUN IN THE FIELD	91-108

LETTER		PAGE
IX.	ON KILLING GAME, AND SHOOTING GENERALLY, IN A SPORTSMANLIKE MANNER	109–126
X.	ON CORRECT AIMING—PRACTICAL	127–138
XI.	ON CORRECT AIMING—PRACTICAL (*continued*)	139–151
XII.	CORRECT AIMING (*continued*)—THEORETICAL (INTENDED TO BE MORE CURIOUS THAN INSTRUCTIVE	152–163
XIII.	SOME REMARKS ON CORRECT AIMING, IN REGARD TO THE EYES	164–172
XIV.	ON THE CARE AND CLEANING OF GUNS—(THEIR LIABILITY TO DAMAGE, AND GENERAL SUPERVISION)	173–188
XV.	THE CARE AND CLEANING OF GUNS (*continued*)	189–197
XVI.	ON THE LOADING OF GAME-GUNS—POWDER	198–205
XVII.	ON THE LOADING OF GUNS—SHOT	206–220
XVIII.	A FEW SIMPLE DIRECTIONS IN TARGET EXPERIMENTS, SUCH AS MAY BE OF USE IN TESTING THE EXCELLENCE, OR THE REVERSE, OF A GUN'S SHOOTING	221–242
XIX.	CARTRIDGES—CARTRIDGE-MAGAZINE—CARTRIDGE-BAG—SLEEVELETS FOR CARTRIDGE-CARRIERS OUT SHOOTING—GAME-BAG	243–253
XX.	GAME-STOP—HOW TO MAKE RABBITS LIE OUT, AND HOW TO CATCH WOOD-PIGEONS	254–263

LETTERS TO YOUNG SHOOTERS

LETTER I

REMARKS ON GUNS OLD AND NEW

MUZZLE-LOADING GUNS (FLINT AND DETONATOR)

To those who recollect the guns of but a score years ago the modern fowling-piece does indeed seem a perfect weapon—so perfect, that it is difficult to imagine in what direction any improvements could be added. Doubtless, however, when the 'detonator' succeeded the 'flint-gun' much the same remark was made. How our ancestors primed, and swore, and primed again, after a missfire with a flint ignition, can readily be guessed. How they turned the flint, screwed it tight, and probed the touch-hole with a long pin kept for emergencies in the corner of the waistcoat; and how they wiped and cleaned the pan, to induce the gun to fire, especially when a woodcock was marked down, and, during rain and snow, held the lock under their coat tails to avoid a certain missfire, has often been described.

Yet, what true and earnest sportsmen they were, all the same; every bit as good as we are now, both in heart and limb, if not, indeed, better in some respects. What did they care, so long as they pursued a healthy, manly sport, if their guns missfired, or if they had to hold 6 feet forward of a crossing bird at twenty paces, so as to allow for the slow ignition of their day and the interval that occurred between pulling the trigger and the charge leaving the muzzle. In those times there was, no doubt, a pleasure and interest in perfecting the appliances of sport that we cannot enjoy to the same extent; for, on my word, our guns are about as near perfection as possible.

It must be admitted, however, that in days of yore the game was more on a par with the weapons used in its destruction than is at present the case. Partridges then lay close and steady, as there was plenty of shelter for them to hide in: the long-cut stubbles were like young woods in their density; the wide, rough hedges were grand shelters, especially in the nesting-season; and the turnip-seed, sown broadcast instead of in mathematical rows, gave such excellent cover that the birds might almost be trodden on before they would rise, and did not run out at one end of a field as the sportsmen looked over a gate at the other. Grouse, long ago, were ignorant of being driven by an army of men, who, by their numbers and well-drilled line as they march across the heather in modern fashion, flush every bird for half a mile. Now our game is wild, and rises at a distance; and, notwithstanding our far-killing and perfect weapons, and our modern system of driving, it is all we can do to get on even terms with it.

Flint-guns were not good killers, however straight they might have been held; they were decidedly inferior to their successors of the copper cap in this respect. But, as with breechloaders on their first introduction, so was it with detonators—a fierce conflict of opinion arose on the latter superseding the more antiquated flint-guns, cherished as they were by the fine old sportsmen of *their* period.

I have made many experiments with both 'flint and ' copper-cap ' guns, in regard to their qualities of shooting, and have found them far behind a fairly good breechloader with ordinary cylinder barrels, the flint-gun especially; though well able, so far as pattern and penetration were concerned, to drop game dead at the distances at which, in the days of close-rising birds, it was necessary to fire. One of the chief reasons why muzzle-loading guns were inferior to our breechloaders was, that the wadding used in loading them fitted the barrels with comparative looseness, necessitated by their being charged from the muzzle; the effect of this resulting in 'windage,' or a waste of propelling power, through the powder-gases escaping round the wads when the charge was ignited. With breechloaders this fault is one that should not occur, as in their case the wads fit tighter at the breech than at the muzzle.

Certainly, the modern shooter has every possible convenience in the capabilities of his gun. Accuracy of aim is about all that he requires—a great advantage over his ancestors, who were obliged to go through all manner of manipulations with their guns before the skill of actual aiming had to be considered. It is fortunate that the latter attribute cannot be mastered and sold by the gunmakers with the gun, or we should soon see the last of British game.

Although the detonating system, as applied to game-guns, was a great improvement upon its predecessor of the flint ignition, yet, when we look back to the copper cap, what a vast amount of trouble and anxiety the latter entailed! We many of us remember its worries: the hasty fumbling in pockets for the different wads, the caps, the powder, the shot—all neatly and systematically placed in their proper receptacles on starting for the day, with apparent impossibility of confusion, but which, nevertheless, after a few shots, seemed mischievously subject to disarrangement.[1]

[1] One of the most original reasons for preferring breechloaders to muzzle-loaders was once given me by the schoolboy son of a sporting farmer. 'You see, sir,' quoth the youngster, 'I likes a breechloader much more than a muzzle-loader because, if a gun ain't got no ramrod, your father can't lay one across your back when he isn't pleased with you out shooting!'

Then the danger of a muzzle-loader was no small item in the day's sport. We often heard of first barrels exploding while second barrels were loading; of caps being jarred off when hammers were down; of powder-flasks, ignited by sparks, blowing fingers to the four corners of a field; of loaded guns being considered unloaded till a man's head with the top shattered proved the contrary; not to speak of such minor incidents as a ramrod sent flying to the clouds, or into a tree—or a cow! And then the constant anxiety present in the mind of a young or nervous shooter, that his gun was doubly served with powder and shot in one barrel—the result of haste in charging —and the consequent dread with which his next shot was looked forward to, and the possible knock-down blow, or even 'burst,' which might ensue.

MODERN GUNS

But we have changed all that. A child could almost be taught to load a modern gun without risk, for none of the misadventures pertaining to the charging of muzzle-loaders apply to breechloaders; and the only real caution the young shooter need exercise is to guard against causing danger to his companions. *That* possibility remains as evident as ever it did, whether the guns be ancient or modern; for safety is the attribute of the shooter, and not of the gun he carries.

Most modern guns, purchased at a fair cost from well-known makers, shoot equally well if of good manufacture; and the shooter will find little difference between them in this respect, provided the gun he uses is adapted to his strength and figure.

It is when a gun does not fit its owner that it gets a bad name as a performer in the field; and just the reverse if it in every way meets his requirements. The actual pattern and penetration of two good guns chosen at random—one that fits the shooter, and one that does not—are, probably, equally satisfactory if tried at that surest of all tests, a target. Though the shooter may fancy that the one gun kills farther and cleaner than the other, this advantage is really caused by his putting the strongest and thickest cluster of the shot well on the mark he aims at, instead of the weakest and most scattered. In fact, his aim being correct through his gun fitting, he is enabled to hit with the centre of the shot-circle, instead of the outside of it. But more of this presently.

When the breechloader first came into favour, the system was regarded as a wonderful innovation, though the new guns were heavy and clumsy, and were secured with awkward closing levers, and had the ordinary hammers and locks of muzzle-loaders. Cartridges to fit the new guns had almost as much care and invention bestowed upon them as the guns themselves; yet a breechloader of twenty years ago —and, in a minor degree, its cartridge—even though considered well-nigh perfect at that date, was simplicity itself when contrasted with a gun of to-day, with its neatly-contrived and wonderfully clever lockwork, its careful boring, and beautitully-constructed barrels; its strength, safety, and general appearance; and, *above all*, its certain ignition under all circumstances of weather and rough usage.

Before quitting the subject of old and modern guns, it is worthy of notice that it was not till the beginning of the present century that double guns came much into favour. At first they were regarded as unsportsmanlike and dangerous innovations; and I have some amusing and strongly-expressed letters referring to their introduction: but, as with many other improvements in gun-making, so with them, convenience soon conquered prejudice. Another thing worth mentioning is, that shooting at flying game is a much more ancient practice than commonly supposed. I have seen woodcuts in old works on sport, published so far back as two centuries, that depict birds on the wing being killed by shooters.

LETTER II

ON THE QUALITY, MANUFACTURE, AND COST OF MODERN GUNS

CHEAP v. BEST GUNS, WITH GENERAL ADVICE ON THE PURCHASE OF A GUN.

FEW recognise the skill and completeness exemplified in a modern gun; and many shooters, I really believe, would never do so unless they were condemned to shoot for a season with the weapons of their forefathers. There is a class of shooters who merely look upon a gun as a machine to kill with, and do not in the least realise the care, expense, and anxiety bestowed on its construction. These are the people who declaim against guns being needlessly expensive if they cost over a very moderate sum. Knowing nothing of the outlay required to produce excellent workmanship, they fancy a cheap gun of 15l. is, or ought to be, as good a weapon as one of 45l., and, making no allowance for first-class material, clever, and therefore costly, artisanship, they cannot see why the lower-priced article should not be as good as that which costs double, and vow it is 'that rascal the gunmaker' who pockets the balance.

To the casual observer there is hardly any perceptible difference in appearance and handling between a fairly well turned out gun and a really first-class one that costs nearly, if not quite, double. Such a man puzzles his brains as to wherein lies the superiority of the expensive over the cheap weapon; for the one apparently works as well, shoots as well, and looks as handsome an article, as the other.[1]

That there *is* a great and important difference is at once evident to those who have a knowledge of what a gun should be; and any ordinary mechanic trained to gun-making, or even a well-versed amateur, would soon point out a score of details evincing either excellence or the reverse.

The simplicity of a good gun and its fewer parts form one of its strongest recommendations; for it is usually in cheap guns that we see complications in

---

[1] The real truth of the matter is, that the majority of men who patronise cheap guns rarely give them such a test of endurance as would determine their merits, if any.

A cheap, rough gun may last for many seasons if it is put to no more severe strain than 300 or 400 shots a year entail. For this reason a 15*l*. gun *may* meet all the requirements of the sportsman who uses it; and the latter is quite right to purchase his gun to suit his purse and his sport, but is *not* justified in swearing by all his gods that, because his 15*l*. gun suits *him*, and stands without damage a *small* amount of wear and tear, it is equal for all practical purposes to a high-class weapon. If the 15*l*. article experienced as much *work* as is usually bestowed on a best gun, it would soon be evident which was the better of the two!

the fastenings, many pieces doing the work which one piece ought to do.

A first-class gun is always handsome, though useless embellishments are frequently omitted. It balances beautifully, works smoothly, and invariably feels light and handy, as compared with an inferior weapon, when put to the shoulder; the latter being good qualities which are among the chief recommendations of first-class work, as well as some of the most useful attributes that a maker of repute is able to bestow on his guns.

Take, for instance, a cheap gun. On a cursory examination, its screws and pins and springs and pieces seem, to all outward appearance, sound and good—and so they are for very ordinary use; but the same parts of a high-class gun are, practically speaking, thrice as excellent, for they are far better in design and material, and have had much more care and harder tests applied to them during their manufacture and fitting.

As an example, in the rough work of wildfowl shooting afloat I am always obliged to use a really good gun—one on the minutest parts of which I can depend. And I find it is true economy to do so; for it is quite a mistake to imagine that a cheap, rough, strong-looking gun will stand hard usage as well as a highly-finished, though perhaps a more delicate-looking, weapon.

I have often tried cheap guns for wildfowl shooting; but a little rust from salt water, or a tumble or two in a boat, and crack goes a screw-head, or snap flies a spring. The gun is then sent to the maker, who writes word: 'These accidents will happen even with the best guns;' but, for my part, I do not find that they do, or at all events very seldom, and in nothing like the same proportion.

Now as to penetration. A cheap gun will, for a time, shoot nearly as hard as an expensive one; but it will not retain its power, the quality of the metal in its barrels not being good enough to enable it to do so. It is, however, in the matter of regular shooting and a properly spread pattern that the good weapon has such an advantage over its cheaper rival, besides being so far superior in lasting powers; for though the strength and balance and finish of a first-class gun are as perfect as may be, these are *not* its *only* advantages, as its shooting qualities are also of the same high standard of excellence.

Cheap guns are usually sold to suit the pockets or fancies of a certain class of customers who cannot or will not give a high price. Well and good; money is a consideration to most. But this does not equalise a cheap and a costly gun in the matter of value and merit.

A sportsman who purchases a cheap gun is not generally one who gives it hard work in regard to the number of shots he fires. The man who can afford to buy an expensive weapon can generally enjoy good shooting; and he may, likely enough, fire 3,000 to 4,000 shots or more a year from one gun. A very well-made article, you may rest assured, does he require for such wear and tear as this—a trial of endurance that few, if any, cheap guns could stand without necessitating repairs.

We do not grudge an extra 20*l*. for a good horse; and if we knew that additional sum would give us as reliable an animal for the required purpose as money could buy, we should gladly pay, and consider the bargain a fortunate one. Then why not so with a gun, *if* we can afford to act in a similar way? Yet I know rich sportsmen, whose surroundings in the matter of horses, pictures, and other belongings are as costly as they can obtain, and as perfect as money can buy, who would on no account expend over 20*l*. on a new gun; because, for some reason best known to themselves, or, at all events, which they cannot explain, they say 'a gun ought not to cost more.'

Cheap guns are made by the hundred, and sold by the hundred. The artisans employed in their manufacture are inferior craftsmen. Among thoroughly clever workmen there is an *esprit de corps* which forbids them from having anything to do with second-class guns. A workman who is really accomplished in the art of gun-making does his work slowly, and with extraordinary care. I have watched such a man by the day; he will not allow himself to be hurried by his employer, or by anybody else, as good work does not admit of haste. For this reason an unlimited number of best guns cannot be turned out by any gunmaker, however large his staff of *employés*. At most, but a few of his men can be trusted to look to the finishing of best guns, as first-class workmen of long experience are always in demand, and few gunmakers can boast of more than three or four on their premises. This is one of the reasons why a good gun takes so long to complete after the order for it is received; for its parts are not turned out by the dozen, as is the case with guns of cheap make.

BEST GUNS

Let us have a look at what the manufacture of a good gun means, and at the same time bear in mind that it is in every detail constructed with as much care and accuracy as the fittings of a valuable watch. It is tested over and over again, and its materials are chosen with the utmost caution, in view of their lasting and other useful capabilities.

First-class gun-barrels are selected from the very best iron and steel; they are put together with the greatest possible care; and they are bored, finished, and adjusted to a thousandth of an inch. The thought and science bestowed on the barrels alone, before they are perfect, represent the experience of a lifetime; and, as instancing what a first-class artisan in the gun-trade is worth to his employer, it is worthy of remark that no machine or lathe has yet been invented that equals in delicacy or rivals in accuracy the touch of such a man's hand, as applied to his tools when finishing a barrel for its shooting, or when bestowing on it a correct outline. The barrels, roughly attached to the stock, are tried at the range, and brought back, and retouched here and there by clever artificers; then they are tried again, and perhaps altered half a dozen times; and several hundred shots may be fired from them before the workman and his master are satisfied that the gun supports their reputation, and is fit for the purchaser.

To arrange the satisfactory shooting of guns is a very difficult and intricate affair. Out of a score of guns sent to the trial-ground, it is quite possible that not one will shoot as does another, though each is bored to all intents alike. To alter them so as to get their performances up to the same standard of excellence is a matter of great care and expense. This difference between the shooting of guns is not to be wondered at when we consider that the thousandth of an inch of deviation in any part of a barrel may throw it off its shooting; and when we also bear in mind that its boring is regulated by manual labour.

The excellence of gun-barrels depends very much on the amount of care they undergo during the process of forging. A barrel that has not been carefully welded is very likely to show 'greys' and sand-holes in its finished state. The former appear in the form of small specks, and are not of great consequence unless in profusion; but the latter are serious defects, of a dangerous nature. These sand-holes run (like the track of a worm in timber) round or along the barrel, inside the metal; and they are wont, by rusting, to increase in size till, perhaps, a fracture occurs. But a crack in a barrel is worst of all, and is the result of really bad manufacture.

In purchasing a secondhand gun, it is well to minutely examine its barrels with a magnifying glass, and probe with the point of a penknife any lines that look like rust, or any crevices that it is possible may have been levelled up with composition in order to conceal the mischief lying underneath. To detect a crack in a pair of barrels, remove the woodwork, hang the barrels up by a string, and strike them with a piece of hard wood. If sound, they will emit a bell-like ring; if damaged, they give out a comparatively dull or jarring note. I have shot with an 8-bore duck-gun that had a small hole in one barrel a foot from the muzzle; but such a defect, though, of course, much against the shooting of a gun, is of little moment, in the matter of safety, compared with what even the smallest crack would be.

The barrels, however, are only one part of a gun. There are the locks, the breech-fittings, the stock, and the finishing—all, in their way, requiring as much attention.

No part of a gun varies more than its locks.

There are many grades of lockmakers alone—men who make common locks, those who make fairly good, good, and really first-class locks;[1] and so it is with every other detail of a gun. Locks can be purchased from a few shillings up to several guineas a pair ; as likewise can breech-actions, as well as the other numerous parts of a gun. What care and excellent arrangement the locks and mechanism of a good gun require can be guessed by most ; but few realise to what extent these qualities are necessary. The stock of a best gun is most carefully chosen from, perhaps, a hundred rough outlines in walnut ; and, finally, the gun is finished by a real artist in the trade—one who turns his work about, and looks at it on every side, considering what is best and what is not, and who, in fact, puts beauty and merit into every touch he gives it with his tools.

How often have I heard it said by a shooter, that he does not care to pay for the engraving of a good gun. Little does he know that engraving is the cheapest part of the weapon, and that a gun can be smothered with scroll-work for a pound or so, though the artistic outlines seen upon an expensive gun cost more. I should never fear that engraving was put on a first-class gun to hide inferior work ; it is applied

[1] Because the locks are hidden from view, they are none the less of exquisite workmanship in a good gun. In this line of business 'Brazier,' of Wolverhampton, has been justly famous for 100 years or more, though his name is better known to gunmakers than to gun-buyers.

as an ornament and finish—as a frame to a picture. But I always suspect engraving on a cheap weapon, as by such means it is easy to conceal bad fittings and materials.

To sum up. I consider that a high-class gun is about as complete and lasting an article as a shooter can buy, and in the long run it is much the least expensive, though it cost him 40*l.* to 45*l.* He may take it for granted, if it be purchased from a well-known gunmaker, that it represents all that is said of it, and that every part—stock, lock, and barrel—is about as perfect as human ability and lavish, though necessary, expenditure can make it. I therefore strongly recommend a first-class gun, from a good maker, as being the most economical in the end; for it will last well, shoot well, work satisfactorily, and always be a safe and pleasant companion to its owner.

CHEAP GUNS

Now a word concerning cheap guns—those sold, for example, at about 15*l.* In the first place, it is impossible to turn out a gun at this price with profit, and at the same time employ the best workmen and materials, or to spend one tithe of the care and time over its manufacture and shooting that a good gun requires. The barrels consist of inferior metal, and they are bored and ground and fitted by second-rate artisans; they have little time wasted upon them, and are rarely shot at the target, save as an experiment to see if they will shoot at all true or evenly; for they have to be made too fast to allow of time being expended on their performances or finish.

The locks and fittings and breech-actions are made of common iron; and so long as these work in a rough-and-ready sort of way, delicate adjustment is discarded, as requiring too great an outlay of time and cost. The stock of such a gun has little care bestowed upon it; for in this line of gun-making a hundred stocks in the rough may have to be made into a hundred finished ones to avoid a loss. These stocks are often bought in a cheap market, improperly seasoned; hence the gaps that appear in cheap guns round the edges of the metal fittings after a short exposure to hot or cold weather. Even when the gun is first bought, on close inspection cracks may frequently be discovered in the stock filled in with paint and varnish, and pieces of wood put in here and there to replace bad material.

To put it plainly, the above class of gun is made to *sell*, and not to *last*; but is, nevertheless, quite good enough for the shooter who knows nothing of what a gun should do, or of its manufacture. For such a man could never realise how it were possible that the breech-action alone of a good gun can cost as much as an entire gun of inferior make in its finished state; and yet such is the fact.

GENERAL ADVICE ON THE PURCHASE OF A GUN

To any one who cannot afford to give more than a small sum for a gun, and who yet must have a gun of some sort, I would say: Purchase a secondhand one by a good maker, as being the cheapest and most satisfactory arrangement; provided that, on showing it to the maker, he speaks favourably of its history and state of preservation. And bear in mind that, as most people rush open-mouthed after hammerless guns at the present day, many hammer-guns have been sold and discarded for no reason other than a change of fashion; and that there are numbers of excellent weapons to be had for 'a song,' secondhand, which would outlast a dozen cheap hammerless ones.

Regarding the cost of guns we hear and read a great deal of nonsense. It almost seems, at times, as if the owner of a cheap gun abused the more costly one merely because he could not afford its purchase, and was too proud to admit it. And perhaps there is a little, too, in the principle of the 'grapes being sour'; for no amount of argument will make bad workmanship on an equality with good. Yet the old, trite statements are daily made, and many shooters still inquire, in injured tones, 'What is the use of going to a first-class gunmaker and giving a high price, when a gun every bit as good can be obtained from a second-class maker at a low figure?

What is the position of a first-class maker? It is this: he will not—in fact, he dare not—sell a gun that is not as perfect as modern science can make it; or where would his reputation and custom be? These would soon crumble to pieces. The result is that shooters, though they pay such a tradesman 20*l.* more than they do a comparatively unknown maker, receive the full value of the extra cost in the satisfaction of knowing they have as good a gun as money can buy, or it would not be sold to them.

I have made many and careful inquiries as to the actual cost a good gun puts its maker to before he offers it for sale. I have gone into and considered every part of a gun—the cost of material and wages of workmen, and the outlay expended in all details of filing, boring, fitting, stocking, screwing, and finishing —and I can state that, on every gun sold by a really good maker at 40*l.* to 45*l.*, a *much* smaller profit than is generally supposed is his perquisite. I can also assure the young sportsman that the profit on a 16*l.* gun is about the same as on the more costly one. Which is the better bargain I leave him to conjecture.

If a shooter cannot afford to give more than a moderate sum for a gun, it cannot be helped; and I have endeavoured to advise him on that point. If, however, he cannot hear of a good secondhand gun, I should recommend him to procure his new gun straight from Birmingham, where cheap goods are the fashion, and where this class of article is made

II. GENERAL ADVICE ON PURCHASING A GUN

stronger and better than in London. Or, to put it plainer, a fairly good weapon is sold at a lower price in that town than it is in London, for a London maker is loth to recommend a second-rate article. In Birmingham, a shooter should obtain a safe, useful gun for 20*l*., which may prove a faithful servant, if not a very polished or accomplished one; and he will find it well worth his while, if within reasonable distance, to choose the gun himself, and see that it fits him—the expense of the journey will not be thrown away.

If the shooter can afford from 40*l*. to 45*l*. for a gun, London is the place to purchase it; for the *very* best class of Birmingham work is decidedly inferior to the *very* best class of London work. It is a general, though erroneous, idea that *all* London gunmakers have their guns sent to London from their Birmingham factories in a finished state and ready for sale. It is true a *large* proportion of so-called London guns *are* made and finished in Birmingham, even down to the name of the seller of the gun in London, and his address. Yet, though they may be few in number, still the best—that is, the *élite*—of the workmen in the gun-trade, or any other trade either, from tailors to tinkers, live and work in London, whatever may be said to the contrary; and hence the fine work of that city, when *done* in that city, as compared with other towns. Without being invidious, I may say that the 'king of the gunmakers' is still Mr. Purdey; and that he, Mr.

Grant, Mr. Holland, Mr. Boss, Mr. Woodward, Mr. Lancaster, Mr. Baker, Mr. Dougall, Mr. Rigby, and Messrs. Cogswell & Harrison, do all their best work in London or its district.

LETTER III

HAMMER, HAMMERLESS, AND EJECTOR GUNS

(WHAT THEY SHOULD DO, AND WHAT THEY SHOULD *NOT* DO)

A GUN with outside hammers and the accompanying old-fashioned side locks has one great advantage, and that is, its simplicity and little chance of going out of order. A hammer-gun is also easily repaired by any ordinary gunmaker or his assistant, and the hammers are plain indications of the gun's safety, or the reverse. I should, therefore, decidedly prefer a cheap hammer-gun to a cheap hammerless, as being the most reliable by reason of its simple construction; and if foreign sport is intended, I should strongly advise hammer-guns alone being taken.

At the same time, I believe a young shooter is less liable to mischance with a hammerless than he is with a hammer-gun, if the former is well made. In a hammer-gun there are several movements to go through, which in wet or cold always require care. In a hammerless, one easy motion should ensure perfect safety.

HAMMER-GUNS

All hammer-guns are now fitted with rebounding locks—that is, the hammers never touch the strikers, or they, in their turn, the caps of the cartridges, except when the triggers are purposely pulled. I am convinced the system of rebounding locks is one of the safest inventions ever applied to guns, and one that has saved many an accident; and, as a secondary consideration, it adds greatly to the speed of loading, as it saves the time that would otherwise be lost in half-cocking.

In old days, if a shooter in the act of cocking his gun allowed the hammer to slip from his thumb, it fell directly on the striker, and 'bang' went the gun. A rebounding lock prevents this risk; as, if the lock is properly made, a hammer should not be able to fire a cartridge unless it be let down from full-cock by the trigger freeing it.

Owing to its simplicity, a hammer-gun can be sold cheaper than a hammerless; and, for this reason, the shooter who can but afford a moderate figure should purchase the former. If a shooter has but 20*l.* to spend, he should certainly choose a hammer-gun; and he may obtain for that sum a better, stronger, and more reliable weapon than the same amount expended on a hammerless.

Hammer-guns are now made much neater than formerly; the hammers are smaller, and lie flatter when the gun is cocked, and are not seen in the act of firing. They *can*, however, be too small; and often are. They are *then* liable to slip from the fingers in very cold weather, or with thick gloves. The hammers should be broad and rough on the comb—or part that comes against the thumb—to enable them, though small and neat, to be at the same time capable of safe manipulation. As to shooting with a hammer-gun, handling them smartly is, after all, only a question of practice. The two best shots in England both use hammer-guns; and, goodness knows, these gentlemen fire their guns quickly enough![1]

HAMMERLESS GUNS

Hammerless guns, before the advent of ejectors, were considered the acme of perfection; and so they are now, if well made; for what are termed ejectors are but hammerless guns with the addition of ejecting mechanism. A *good* hammerless of the present day is about as perfect an article as a shooter could desire to possess; yet it is only within the past five or six years that these guns have generally become reliable. A few seasons ago, and the owner of a 'hammerless' was always sent first over a stile or through a hedge, as these weapons not seldom exploded without warning, or failed in some less dangerous manner.

Now, every gunmaker of note has his own par-

[1] Earl de Grey and Lord Walsingham.

ticular 'bantling' in the form of a special gun, christened with what he considers a taking name—which often suggests that his gun is alone, of all others, the safest and best; though their patents are nearly all modifications or downright imitations of the original invention of Messrs. Anson & Deely, to whom honour is due as the earliest to introduce good weapons of this description to the public. When first invented, hammerless guns were extremely complicated, and, from their numerous parts and dependent mechanism, often signally failed in use; but latterly gunmakers have greatly simplified the construction of these guns, and have reduced to a minimum the number of pieces their locks contain—of course, adding much to their success and safety thereby.

A good hammerless gun may now be relied on to fire 5,000 shots a season for years without requiring repairs; and if it is capable of such a hard strain as *this* entails, I do not see much more need be required of it. The locks may run many years without repair, and with very slight supervision in the way of cleaning—and I have good proof of this in my own guns.

'Hammerless' are as safe as guns can be, provided they are fitted with a reliable intercepting block that is always between the hammers and the cartridge—a safeguard that protects the gun from discharge by a fall or jar, and which is only removed by the shooter pulling the triggers. The first question a young shooter should satisfy himself upon is whether the gun he proposes to purchase, if it be a hammerless, *has* this block; and let him have nothing to do with it should it be without such a vitally important protection from accident.

In purchasing a hammerless gun—even supposing it to be absolutely reliable and safe in every respect —there are other secondary qualities to be looked for. It should work evenly, and without any perceptible jerk, or undue exercise of leverage, in opening or shutting; else it will be found a slow gun to load in a hurry, and not so quick as a hammer-gun in this respect. It should easily and smoothly do the work of compressing the mainsprings in cocking; and, on turning the opening lever, the barrels should drop down of themselves to receive the cartridges. They should do this almost as freely as those of a hammer-gun, and without any noticeable pressure on them from the left hand of the shooter—a pressure which means waste of time in loading.

The gun should open to the extent of at least an eighth of an inch between the top of the false breech and the lower edge of the extractors. A gun that opens like this always does its work best; for, from the barrels falling well down, it obtains plenty of leverage to divide the work of cocking over a considerable space, and the power then used to compress the springs is scarcely felt. When a gun opens but a slight distance it feels stiff and heavy in the act of cocking, as its mainsprings have to be compressed by a short and cramped movement, instead of by a long, easy one.

Many hammerless guns are so constructed that their barrels only just drop clear of the breech. A shooter has then to carefully notice his gun every time he loads, to see if it is far enough open for him to insert a fresh cartridge. Some gunmakers leave this opening space so narrow that, unless the barrels are held perfectly level, and at their lowest angle, the rim of the cartridge-case will catch against the top edge of the breech, either in loading or unloading. Of course, a gun on these lines is faulty; for it is difficult to load and fire it as fast as a few quick shots may at any time necessitate. A hammerless gun should open well clear of the breech; there is then no difficulty in placing the fingers, however cold, well round the cartridges to pull them out, or, if necessary, to enable an extractor to be applied with full force. At the same time, the shooter should be careful to choose a gun that cocks before it can be re-loaded, or else the locks might not be fully cocked when he wishes to fire.

In all hammerless guns the springs are compressed when the gun is shut and ready for use; and, as gunmakers cannot well alter this state of things, they tell us compressed springs are of no consequence. That this is not the case stands to reason; therefore, at the end of the day, invariably insert dummy cartridges fitted with springs in their centres, and pull the triggers. Empty cases should never be used for this purpose, as the strikers drive into the caps after a few blows, and the points of the former are then liable to wear and tear from the force required to free them on opening the gun.

The sliding stud that moves the trigger-safety of a hammerless gun should be fairly large; it is then convenient to the touch. It is often made too small, and safety and utility are sacrificed to unnecessary neatness. This safety stud should be large enough to be felt and manipulated easily with the thickest gloves or the most benumbed fingers; and, for my part, I should prefer one that required a downward as well as a sliding pressure, as a precaution against accidental movement.

Of the various fastenings a gun requires to connect the barrels and stock I will presently treat. I will now speak of ejectors.

EJECTOR GUNS

These are hammerless guns fitted with extractors, which, by means of springs, jerk out the exploded cartridges. Here we have the last improvement in guns, and one that is not yet perfected.

Every gunmaker has, of course, his own simply infallible ejector, and, according to him, the only one in the trade that really works properly. It is not, however what a picked gun in a shop will do in the hands of its inventor; it will *there* jerk out the cartridges with force enough to put your eye out or break the windows. What one requires to know is, what the gun will do in the field with hard usage. I write 'hard usage' advisedly, for a gun must stand that or nothing, as we do not want guns that require extra care or moderate use. They must all be—to use a school phrase—as 'hard as nails,' and fit for anything. There are only a few really reliable ejectors in the market at present, and which do their work in a manner that defies criticism; and I consider the best are those of Mr. Purdey, Mr. Holland, Mr. Greener, Messrs. Westley-Richards (Deely's patent), Mr. Lancaster,[1] Mr. Woodward, Mr. Grant, Mr. Boss, Messrs. Cogswell & Harrison, Messrs. Rigby, and last, certainly not least in its excellence, Mr. Maleham's.

That ejectors are the guns of the future there is not the slightest doubt; for a shooter is quite as ready to appreciate and patronise a decided convenience as any one else. If a shooter can afford 40*l*. to 45*l*., by all means let him purchase an ejector, as for this price he should be able to get a good one. I do not believe a less sum could purchase one such as I should

---

[1] Though Mr. Lancaster's guns are most admirably turned out— none better—and his 'ejector' is as good as any, it is only fair to state that the mechanism of the latter, as well as of many other 'ejectors,' is the invention of Mr. Perkes, of 14 Castle Street, Berners Street, London, who deserves praise for contriving so simple and reliable an 'ejecting action,' and one which can be fitted to almost any hammerless gun by the substitution of a new fore-end.

care to recommend; for 'ejectors' are still in their infancy, as far as the trade of gun-making generally is concerned, or they would be sold at a more moderate sum than is now the case.

A well-made ejector—one that works smoothly, and does not require more leverage to cock it than an ordinary hammerless—can, without doubt, be loaded and fired with great rapidity; so fast, indeed, that a dozen shots in quick succession out of each barrel would make the gun too hot to hold.

The great advantage of an ejector is, that a man who uses but one gun can, if occasion demand, shoot nearly as fast as if he had two guns and a loader. This, of course, means bagging more game. And it is no very difficult feat for a shooter armed with an ejector to drop three partridges, one by one, out of a covey rising near him—so quickly can he reload.

But an ejector needs be very perfect in every detail; and it is no advantage that it can be used as an ordinary gun should its ejecting mechanism fail—an alternative sometimes described by its inventor as a recommendation. If we give an extra price for an ejector, we expect it to act as one, and not as an ordinary hammerless; and a statement of this kind implies a want of faith on the part of the maker of the gun in regard to its reliability.

Most ejectors, however well they eject, have one decided disadvantage; and that is, they do not withdraw unfired cases far enough for the shooter conveniently to unload with cold fingers, or to enable him to extract a case which is at all tight. Many ejectors do not draw back a loaded case more than a sixteenth to an eighth of an inch, which gives a very small edge for the fingers to grasp, particularly if the barrels have dolls'-heads, or other unsightly projections to take up space, and shut out the base of the cartridge from the fingers when it is wished to withdraw the former. The extractors of an ejector should project, when the gun is opened in an unfired state, a full quarter of an inch. Messrs. Purdey's ejectors are particularly good in this respect.[1]

When about to purchase an ejector, be careful to ascertain that, if the barrels compress the mainsprings on opening, the locks are cocked *before* the cartridges are ejected. Open the gun very slowly, and you will hear the locks cock by the clicking sound they give, either before or after the cartridges are jerked out, as the case may be. This is important in an ejector, as the fact of the cartridges being ejected gives, especially to an assistant, the idea that the gun may be closed, and is ready for use.

For this reason I prefer an ejector that cocks as

[1] Not long since, when examining an ejector, and pointing out what a slight distance its extractors withdrew the unfired cases, I was told, with an air of triumph: 'The great advantage of an ejector, sir, is that you never require to unload, as the gun does that for you.' This is all wrong; for a man who values his life, as well as the lives of others, will *frequently* have to unload in a day's shooting; and assuredly this act should be as easy in its performance as it can be made.

the barrels are closed, after the cases are ejected; there can then be no possible doubt about the gun being ready for firing. Perhaps the best ejector of all is the one that half-cocks its locks on opening the breech, and full-cocks them on closing it. The gun that does this divides its work very evenly, and is pleasant in use, as no particular exercise of strength is required to charge it; and it can certainly be fired and reloaded faster than can a gun that compresses its springs in the one motion of either opening or closing.

LETTER IV

ON THE FIT AND CHOICE OF A GUN, AND THE BEST GUN TO USE AS ADAPTED TO DIFFERENT SHOOTERS

THE FIT OF A GUN

IN the actual choice of a gun, irrespective of its qualities and mechanism, there is a good deal of judgment required. A would-be purchaser may enter a shop, and take up gun after gun till he has handled a score, and yet feel conscious—though he cannot tell why—that he has not even then had in his hands a gun that seems to come up to his shoulder and eye as pleasantly and satisfactorily as he is confident it should do if it really suited him.

A clever gunmaker, who has made a specialty of fitting guns, and has really succeeded in doing so, tells by instinct as much as by rule the kind of weapon to offer to individual shooters: he can note the attitudes and detect the faults of a shooter's position far better than can the handler of the gun himself; and if the latter had a hundred guns from amongst which to select, unassisted, a suitable bend and cast-off adapted to his figure, he might doubt and hesitate, and in the end, perhaps, be no better off than when he began to pick and choose; though a gunmaker, if an adept at fitting a gun, would at once put his customer on the road to success. Therefore, if possible, always get fitted with a gun by an accomplished gunmaker; and when *he* tells you the gun fits, and *you* feel and prove that it does so, you may rest content.

It is of as much importance to a shooter that his gun should fit him, as it is for it to shoot well; as, however well a gun may shoot, this good quality cannot be taken advantage of unless, in the first place, the gun is adapted to its user. It is impossible for the best of shots to aim correctly if his gun misfits him; how much more such a deficiency would affect a bad or even a moderate marksman may be imagined.

The broad principle of trying a gun's fit is for the shooter to *fling*[1] it quickly up from the hip to the shoulder, and, without the slightest hesitation, aim at a small mark level with the eye some few yards distant. If he finds the sight comes fair on the mark

---

[1] I purposely write *fling*, as this word implies just what a man should do with his gun when about to fire at game, or even test it at a target to see if it fits him. A good, quick marksman seldom *aims*, in the sense of drawing a sight on his bird—he has no time to do so; he *flings* his gun to the shoulder, directing it towards the game he desires to kill, without really sighting his mark, or looking for the muzzle of the gun. *If* his gun fits him *perfectly*, the shooter will find that, by merely pointing the barrels at an object, the sight will come up to his wishes almost without fail, whether in daylight or dusk. It is usually the man who closes one eye who takes the steady aim that, from the time expended thereon, so often results in a miss behind at a crossing shot.

time after time, without the aim requiring any correction, at the moment the gun reaches the shoulder, it will not be, at all events, a bad fit, whatever its shape; and though the shooter may not be able to kill as well with the gun as he might do with a still better-fitting one, he will not shoot badly, taking into consideration, of course, his powers of marksmanship and eye. But the gun needs to come up, when put to the shoulder, straight on the mark chosen, whether the latter be high, low, right, left, or centre.

The shooter should snap one lock the instant he sights the mark, and notice if his aim is thereby diverted, as the pull-off of the trigger often affects the steadiness of the muzzle if the former is not suited to the hand and finger of the sportsman.

The best object to aim at is a black seal, 1 inch in diameter, set in the centre of a piece of white card, 8 inches square, with a red seal in each of its corners. The shooter can then readily discover, when aiming quickly, if the sight of his gun comes up fair on the centre seal, or if it rests on either corner of the card, high or low, to one side or the other.

A little practice of this kind, when trying a gun, is of immense advantage, as it is obvious that, however good or bad a shot a man may be, if his gun does not point accurately on the object he aims at he is obliged to alter his sight—in fact, to readjust it; and slow shooting is the natural result of taking two sights instead of one.

THE FIT OF THE STOCK OF A GUN

It is worth remembering that, if a gun, on being put quickly to the shoulder and snapped—

(1) Points too *low*, or under the mark, then the stock of the gun is either too short for the shooter or too much bent.

(2) If it points *high*, the stock is too straight.

(3) If the gun points to the *right*, the stock is cast-off too much to the right.

(4) If to the *left*, it has not sufficient cast-off to the right.

Though the stocks of guns have to be bent—some much, some little—to match the figure of the shooter, he should recollect that, the straighter a stock he can use, the quicker and more accurate will be his aim, especially in regard to all overhead shots or driven game. A long-armed or tall man generally requires a gun with a long stock and well bent; and a short man, a short and straight stock. A broad-chested man requires a stock with a fair amount of cast-off to the right, so as to bring the barrels to the left, and in line with his sight, instead of his having to bring his face to the stock, as would be his case with a gun without sufficient cast-off to the right. A narrow-chested man will require very little cast-off, as his stock will be nearer to his face, and the barrels naturally more in line with his eyes.

Though there are shooters whose marksmanship does not improve, whatever alterations be made to their guns, yet there is many a bad shot whose powers of aiming correctly can often be much assisted by merely altering the slope of the butt of his gun at the heel, as well as by regulating the cast-off of the stock to his figure.

If a gun shoots low, the slope of its heel can be straightened with good effect. If it shoots too high, the heel can be sloped more than it is, and the gun thereby caused to come up level with the eye in consequence of the alteration. But all this requires to be done with great care and judgment, and most cautiously, as a very little shaping of the heel makes a great deal of difference in the fit of the gun.

When trying a gun, allow the coat to be buttoned close and smooth over the chest. Out shooting, a thin patch of leather on the shoulder is of great service, and much assists in bringing the butt tightly and evenly to the figure. Bear in mind, too, that a gun does not really fit unless its entire butt comes fair and square, in all positions of aiming, against the hollow of the shoulder; for, the better and more truly the butt fits the shoulder, the more comfortable will the gun be in use, and the less will its recoil be felt.

I have heard a shooter laughingly exclaim that he could not shoot on such a day because he was wearing his winter gun with his summer coat. This seems absurd; but still there is a certain amount of truth in the idea, as a thin coat might appear to appreciably shorten the stock of a gun, while a thick coat would have a reverse effect.

The balance of a gun has also a good deal to do with the recoil, for a badly-balanced gun will always recoil more than one that is well balanced. Most cheap guns are very inferior in the matter of balance, their muzzles being too heavy and strong—a sign of rough workmanship, as the weight should be at the breech, not at the muzzle; the latter only requires to be strong enough to resist indentation.

Another thing which affects recoil is the handle of the stock of a gun. In a common gun it is round, and hence feels loose and clumsy, and the stock is apt to turn in the hand, when the gun is put to the shoulder, as a result. The handle of a gun should be egg-shaped in its cross-section; this part requires careful finishing, but, when well designed, gives a comfortable grasp and a firm and easy position to the right hand; for if the handle of a gun is thus correctly shaped, it assists the shooter, as it causes the butt to come evenly against his shoulder, and enables him to keep the gun level when taking aim.

A bruised arm and face are sure to result if the butt of a gun does not sit properly against the chest; and this is particularly the case when the top of its heel projects over the top of the shooter's shoulder.

A gun that fits a shooter well requires less exertion to aim with, and appears to weigh lighter, than one that does not. It is this important attribute of fitting a gun that our best makers succeed in bringing to such perfection when a customer gives them the opportunity of doing so; and it is hard upon a gunmaker's reputation when he does not have the chance of obtaining success in this important part of his business. Of course, hundreds of guns are ordered straight from London or Birmingham without a trial of any kind; sometimes they fit, and more times they do not; and the consequence is, that a gun is often blamed as a poor performer in the field merely because it does not suit its owner's figure, and, as a result, he is unable to shoot straight with it.[1]

It is not an unusual custom for a shooter to select from the guns he sees in a shop one which *he* thinks fits him; he then orders an exact copy, and in due course this is sent home. It has then to be taken for better or for worse; it may give satisfaction, or it may not, though with practice it will probably fairly well meet his requirements. On the other hand, the

[1] A London gunmaker has immense experience in the matter of different and unusual eyesight, as he is brought into frequent contact with sportsmen who describe their peculiarities in this respect with a view to correction. London has a great advantage over Birmingham in this matter; but I must not say too much, or we shall have the gunmakers of the latter town sitting in solemn conclave to assure us that a man's eyesight can be judged from his handwriting.

shooter may consider the mechanism and requisite capabilities of his gun in the first place, and trust to his *gunmaker* fitting the gun to him properly when it is near completion—the latter being the best method to adopt.

If a shooter is abroad, and wishes to have an exact copy of a favourite gun, let him lay it on a thin, smooth board, and trace its outline in pencil, afterwards cutting the model out with a fine saw. This is far better than trusting to measurements, which may be right, and may be wrong. The model can be cut in half, or even in three pieces, with a view to portability by post; and at the time it is forwarded to the gunmaker, measurements of the shooter's height, length of arm, and especially his chest measurement across the shoulders, should be included, so as to give an idea of the amount of cast-off required in the stock.

There is no extra expense to a shooter in having his gun made to fit him properly; and care in this respect is amply repaid after purchase. If a shooter is conscious his gun is all that it should be in its fit and performances, he knows that any fault of marksmanship lies apart from the gun, and by practice and perseverance may be cured. On the other hand, if he has reason for doubting the quality and suitability of his gun, he is inclined, and perhaps rightly, to blame wood and iron more than hand and eye.

Most gunmakers have private ranges at which to try guns. A shooter should visit one of these, and aim and fire quickly a series of shots at a black bull's-eye in the centre of a 4 ft. square white target, and after each discharge carefully notice if the centre of the shot-circle covers the mark; till *this* occurs the gun does not suit him.

The distance in these experiments can be thirty paces, so that the outline of the circle made by the shot may be well defined. Before commencing, the gun may be fired fair on the bull's-eye, as if it were a rifle, to see if it acts its part and places the charge from each barrel accurately; for if the gun does not perform as it should, all endeavours on the part of the shooter will be so much time wasted.

When firing at a target with a new gun, it is well to discover, on discharging the right barrel, if the muzzle flies upwards to an undue extent—though it always will do so more or less. A friend looking on can see if this occurs; and the shooter can himself ascertain if it does by firing both barrels rapidly in succession at the same mark, without taking the gun down from the shoulder, and then noticing whether the pattern of the second shot is placed clear of the first one; if the latter occurrence takes place, the gun jumps too much in the shooter's grasp, from being a bad fit.

It is curious, to say the least, that a shooter will often adhere to one style of stock in his gun all his life. When he buys a new gun, off goes an old one to be copied exactly, because it fitted him a score years before.

He then wonders why on earth he does not shoot with his new gun as well as he did with his old one of long ago, and the gunmaker is dubbed a careless fellow. The shooter, perhaps, omits to consider that, in the course of years, *his* outline is changed—which necessitates a changed outline in the stock of his gun—and that the latter will require to be adapted to the alteration in his figure as much as does the fit of his clothes. The tailor is given a chance of doing this, whilst the gunmaker is overlooked. The very best contrivance ever devised for discovering the style of gun that is most suitable to a shooter, whatever his figure or eyesight, is Jones's 'Try Gun.' This capital invention is a gun that can be altered by a twist here, and a screw there, to any variety of shape in regard to cast-off, slope of stock, bend, and so forth. As a natural result, a shooter can blaze away with this article either at live birds or at a target till his success shows him the try gun fits him. All that is then necessary is a new gun, or his old stock altered to the same shape—an easy matter. Let any young shooter give a call in at Mr. Henry Holland's, 98 New Bond Street, and see this 'dodge'; it is worth a visit.

THE SELECTION OF A GUN IN REGARD TO ITS WEIGHT AND CHARGE

I have so far spoken of the choosing of a gun in regard to its fit; but a good deal has to be considered concerning the best gun for a shooter to use in the field in relation to his powers of aiming, his strength, and the description of sport he expects to enjoy. A gun, whether it be the usual 12-bore or a smaller size, may, as far as mere fit goes, suit equally well; but the shooter has to consider many things besides this very necessary feature of his gun. For instance, if a shooter is not of a strong build, he should carry a gun to match his strength—one that, when he is a little tired, does not seem as if the barrels had a lump of lead at the muzzle when put up for a shot. There is no surer sign of a gun being too heavy than if, at the end of the day, the muzzle points under the mark, or when, on bringing it to the shoulder in the evening, it seems a pound or two heavier than it did in the morning.

A gun that is in the least degree too heavy for the arms of a shooter is a sad failure, and implies incorrect aiming for the latter half of the day at least; and I strongly advise a young shooter, in purchasing a new gun, to put it to his shoulder many times in succession, in order to discover whether he can keep its muzzle on the mark he aims at when his arms are more or less fatigued.

A shooter should be able to put his gun up and down correctly at a mark quite thirty times as rapidly as he can go through the movements of aiming and shouldering; and with a little practice he may do so as many as forty times; though it takes quite an athlete to do so fifty times (try, and see!) Placing the actual fit of your gun out of the question, you will find such exercise as this, if regularly repeated, of *great* advantage in strengthening the arms, and enabling you to bring your gun in line with anything you direct it towards.

If a gun is too heavy for a man's strength at first, it will always be so, especially in regard to quick aiming—which means placing the muzzle fair on the game, or the point chosen by the eyes, directly the gun is put to the shoulder.

Of course, where money is not an object, a shooter can, if he wishes, possess several guns. For instance, a friend of mine uses a light gun in August and September for walking up partridges or young grouse, with or without dogs; he uses a still lighter one for rabbits; a fairly heavy gun for grouse-driving, and one still more powerful for hares, pheasants, wood-pigeons, or ducks. In the case of men who have a good deal of shooting, a pair of guns are often in use at the same time. So that a very extensive and costly outfit might easily be selected, and yet all the guns brought into use, on different occasions, by those sportsmen whose pockets are well filled, and who, taking a pleasure in possessing a regular 'armoury,' do not mind carrying guns of unequal weights at different seasons of the year.

But for average sport, a pair of guns, or even one gun if but an occasional day's shooting be indulged in, is amply sufficient: so that a good general gun or pair of guns for all-round sport throughout the season is what most people need consider. For my part, I am convinced that a shooter should avoid using guns of varied weights on game, as nothing is more likely to put him off his shooting than so doing; and whether he has six guns or a pair, each and all should balance and fit just the same, so that no divergence can be detected when putting them to the shoulder; else an uncertain aim, and, of course, indifferent shooting, may be the result.

I certainly recommend on all occasions a 12-bore, whether the gun requires to be light or heavy, or whether small, moderate, or full charges have to be fired. Depend upon it, this size is far the most useful one for every bird or animal, in our game list or out of it, which we are accustomed to meet with during an ordinary day's sport; and that a 12-bore can be adapted to any shooter's requirements I am equally confident.

Guns of 16-, 20-, and 28-bore always handle and feel pleasant, especially in a gunmaker's shop, and give the idea that they must be easy to hit with as a natural consequence; but from numerous experiments, both at the target and in the field, I can positively state that any bore smaller than a 12 is not so effective on game, nor so easy to aim straight with, as the latter size. Small-gauge barrels of necessity shoot weaker than a larger size: they have a more open pattern if cylinders, and a closer if chokes; they do not shoot so regularly, and, in proportion, recoil more than do 12-bores. Of course, a 16 comes nearest to a 12; but even a 16 has these disadvantages, though on a lesser scale than a 20—the latter being the favourite weapon of the small-bore shooter.

I will therefore take a 20 as an example; for not only do the patrons of these guns vow they kill as well as a 12-bore, but, some people will tell you, even better. Until, however, I can be persuaded that black is white, or the reverse, I will never believe that a 20, firing a charge of three-quarters, or even seven-eighths of an ounce of shot, can possibly rival in effectiveness a 12-bore gun firing an ounce, or an ounce and an eighth; any more than that a half-pound weight dropping on one's toes can strike with as much force as a weight of three-quarters of a pound.

There is, in every charge of shot fired from a 12-bore, always a number of pellets that diverge, and are, as a result, weak in regard to their striking force. In the case of a 20-bore there are still more; and, from the charge being smaller, the 20 can, least of the two, afford to waste any pellets, if its pattern is to be a serviceable one.

When a charge of shot is fired from a gun, the top pellets, being farthest from the powder, obtain the least propelling power, and are chiefly driven out by the pellets behind them, and so cannot be relied on for regularity of flight and velocity. Consequently, the closer the shot lies to the wads over the powder, the stronger are the pellets propelled; and it is easy to see that, the smaller the bore of a gun, the more elongated in proportion is the charge of shot, and the farther from the powder will the upper half of the charge lie; hence the larger average of weak and wasted pellets in a small-bore gun.

A small-bore gun, on account of the narrowness of its barrels, is never so easy to aim with as one of larger size and, of course, greater width; and the more like aiming with a rifle, or a single-barrelled gun, is the natural result.

Provided it is aimed perfectly true, a shooter may place enough pellets into his game to kill it at 40 yards with a *full-choked* 20, or even 28, if the penetration of his gun is equally satisfactory. But the former is no easy feat to perform regularly, and the latter attribute the gun cannot attain to the same extent as a 12-bore.

How often have I heard and read of shooters who state that they have killed their game time after time with a 20 as well and far as any one could do with a 12-bore, and who carefully quote, in support of such imaginary performances, the occasional long shots they have made. All I can say is, I have never seen a 20 nearly equal a 12 for efficiency, though I have tried this bore often enough. But with a 20-bore I have seen game regularly and constantly wounded that, if struck with a 12, would have dropped dead. Often, too, have I heard a man shooting with a 20 say, 'I can't imagine how I missed that bird,' when I had noticed that he had not missed his bird, but had in reality wounded it.

It is worth remark that No. 5 shot contains too few pellets to the ounce for the charge of a 20-bore (unless the gun is a full-choke); and gunmakers, as well as those who use these small weapons, admit that, in order to obtain a fair pattern, No. 7 shot is best suited to their capabilities. Now, if a man wishes to wound at a long range, and spoil game at a short one, he could not choose a more suitable size than this.

I do not deny that a 20-bore will kill birds well enough early in the season at moderate distances; but I most emphatically declare that, for fairly wild game, a 20-bore does not approach a 12 in general usefulness or excellence. As to a 28, I merely regard it as a contrivance to wound, save when used on game at a short range; and a gun that will only kill well at a short range, and wounds at a fairly long one, is *not* the class of weapon a shooter ought to carry.[1]

In regard to all small-bores, it should be remembered that long shots now and then go for nothing; they are but chances that occur with any gun, as a very long shot may merely result from one random pellet chancing to take its flight into the head or

---

[1] I will qualify the above by saying I have found a 28-bore a useful little 'spitfire' for killing water-rats, as well as for bagging small birds to feed my trained hawks with.

heart of a bird; and, to my mind, nothing shows the decided inferiority of small-bores so effectively as a few shots with them at strong, high pheasants or hares crossing at a good distance. It is, in fact, impossible for any shooter of an observant nature and unprejudiced mind not to remark the poor performance of a 20-bore on such occasions, as compared with even a light 12-bore.

It is often said when small-bore guns are discussed, that our ancestors used them successfully. True, so they did; but they used them on the tame birds of long ago—birds that generally rose at nearer 18 than 35 yards; the latter being a usual distance for game to be killed at in the present day when rising in front of the shooter late in the season.

A favourite argument on behalf of small-bores is that, for the old, the weak, or the young, they are, from their lightness, easy to carry. But this argument does not really apply, as, if required, a 12-bore can now be made as light as a 20-bore, and to shoot the same charges as the latter size. This the 12-bores undoubtedly do, with better penetration and pattern, and with less recoil; and, what is more, they are far more easy to aim correctly with, and are also, to a certain extent, safer as well, for the strain on the discharge of a 20 is always more severe than is the case with a 12-bore.

If a shooter requires a light gun, let him select a light 12-bore, and he will shoot better with it than he will with a 20, or even with a 16; and this fact I can with every confidence assert, after countless experiments of my own, and after carefully noting scores of shooters, using all sizes of guns, on all kinds of game.

For a general gun suitable for English game throughout the season, and adapted to an ordinary shooter of fair marksmanship and moderate strength, I should recommend a 12-bore gun of $6\frac{3}{4}$ lb., or a trifle under, with 29 in. barrels, to fire 3 dr. of black powder or 42 gr. of a nitro-compound, the charge of shot $1\frac{1}{16}$ oz. of No. 6.

The gun for a man of weak physique should be one of $6\frac{1}{4}$ lb. weight, 28 in. barrels, the charge a light 3 dr. of black or 40 gr. of nitro-compound, and 1 oz. of No. 6 shot.

For the shooter who cannot carry $6\frac{1}{4}$ lb. with comfort all day, and requires something still lighter, a 12-bore gun can be easily built for him by a good maker weighing $5\frac{3}{4}$ lb., which will be perfectly reliable, and from which he can shoot $2\frac{3}{4}$ dr. of powder and $\frac{7}{8}$ oz. to 1 oz. of No. 6 shot both safely and effectively, the barrels being 27 in. in length. With a gun like this a shooter will be more successful than with a 20-bore of $5\frac{1}{2}$ lb., as the 12-bore will have better penetration and pattern, will come up easier and more accurately to the shoulder, recoil considerably less, and in reality be just as handy and light to carry as the 20. Any one who requires a lighter gun than this had better not shoot, unless he is remorseless in the matter of wounding his game.

A powerful man can use a 12-bore of 7 lb., or a trifle less, shooting 1⅛ oz. of No. 5 or No. 6 shot, and 3¼ dr. of black or 43 to 44 gr. of a nitro-compound. A shooter in good health and of good physique should not feel in the least tired from using a 7 lb. gun, even at the end of a long day's sport; and weight, *when* unfelt, gives an advantage in the matter of strength, recoil, hard hitting, and steadiness of aim.

It is worthy of notice that a shooter will do well to avoid selecting a gun with a pistol-hand. This arrangement is a good one for rifles, as it gives a strong and firm grip, and assists in steadying the aim; but when applied to a shot-gun it is an undoubted mistake, as it confines the right hand too much, and hinders it from moving with the gun, or from quickly grasping it to fire a snap-shot. A pistol-hand is also in another way detrimental to quick shooting, for it prevents the hand slipping back, as is intuitively done by a shooter before he can fire the left trigger— the result being a slow second barrel after a miss with the first.

Let me here remark that, for all-round shooting, there is no advantage whatever in the traditional custom of having one barrel of a gun bored to fire a closer pattern than the other, especially as regards driven game, as in the latter case, taking the shots that offer one with another, there is no constant difference in the ranges at which the birds pass overhead; and, even when walking up partridges or grouse, it generally occurs that the first to rise are the old birds, as they are the wildest, and hence a long shot to the right barrel is as likely as to the left one. Gunmakers seem to imagine that it is the constant habit of game to rise in pairs, and offer a near and then a distant shot in succession to each barrel as fired. If a shooter fired all his life at pigeons sprung from traps, or made it a rule to miss with his first barrel, it would be another matter.

LETTER V

THE CHOICE OF GUNS (continued), *WITH REMARKS ON THEIR FASTENINGS, THE MERITS OF STEEL AND DAMASCUS, AND THE LENGTH OF GUN-BARRELS*

THE MECHANISM OF A GUN

WHEN choosing a gun, a shooter should very carefully examine all the fastenings, large and small, that connect the barrels with the metal-work of the stock, to see if they work smoothly in opening and closing, and, above all, fit perfectly, without any sign of a crevice or symptom of a shake.[1]

As to top fastenings, there are scores of them, of all shapes and sizes, but very few that are of any use; for a good gun can be made just as strong and safe without, and at the same time be more convenient in use, less liable to damage, far easier to repair if necessary, and a handsomer article into the bargain!

Of course, gunmakers who have favourite top-

---

[1] To test a gun to discover if it has any 'shake' in its joints, hold its heel in the palm of the left hand, and, grasping the handle of its stock firmly in the right hand, move the gun several times strongly and quickly from side to side, its barrels directed upwards.

fastenings of their own invention declare no gun is safe without some such addition; but it is rare to see a gun with a doll's-head, extension rib, cross-bolt, or any other unsightly device of the kind, except when it is of Birmingham make, or is sold at a low figure.

The few best London makers who add a top fastening always construct it as small and neat as possible; and if asked why they spoil the look of their guns in this fashion, when they are sufficiently strong without such a disfigurement, will reply: 'We are bound to act thus, as the public fancy that the more fastenings a gun has, the stronger it is'; and that, if a gun had half a dozen 'grips' round the breech, many gentlemen would imagine (they are sometimes told so) that such a gun would be just six times as safe as a gun with one fastening.

Putting three or four extra fastenings to the breech of a gun is like using several threads for a bow-string which do not pull together, instead of one strong string that does; the latter in this case being represented by the usual lumps under the barrels.

The only top fastenings I am aware of which really add strength to a gun in some slight degree are those of Messrs. Westley-Richards and Mr. W. W. Greener. The mechanism of the latter is preferable, but it has the disadvantage that, with rough work, sand or rust stops it from acting freely; and, though liking its principle under conditions favourable to its success, I have for this reason had to discontinue its use at sea, and even on shore when shooting where dust or sand is blown about, as I have several times been unable to close the lever of a cross-bolt gun in the midst of a 'drive' through particles of grit having lodged in the mechanism. At the same time, if a shooter, for some private reason, persists in having a top fastening to his gun, he cannot have a neater-looking one than Mr. Greener's; and I certainly consider that Mr. Greener's guns approach nearer in their general excellence to best London guns than do those of any other provincial maker I am acquainted with.

A cheap gun—one about 15*l.* or so—is very rarely made without a top fastening; not to speak of other unusual grips never seen in a best London, or even a best Birmingham, gun. In a cheap gun the top extension and other intricate devices for holding the barrels to the breech are usually of clumsy appearance; and, of course, when made of *large* size, as is then the case, they are bound to have a certain influence on the strength of the gun, especially when the lumps under the barrels and the barrels themselves are badly fitted and of inferior construction and design. Nevertheless, a gun sold as having several 'grips' may *always* be looked upon as being a second-rate piece of work, that requires an extra amount of strength, real or imaginary, to hold it together.

How often have I heard it asserted that no gun, good or bad, is really safe without a top fastening, and that a gun is far stronger with than without this complex addition! How, would I ask, is it, then, that I, and hundreds of others, who use guns devoid of top fastenings, fire year after year thousands and thousands of shots without these cumbrous contrivances? I confess I like facts; and this is one that is rather to the point. The advocates of top fastenings sometimes give most amusing reasons for their use, such as that they prevent the barrels of a gun springing from the standing breech, or from moving laterally; as if the lumps secured to the barrels, and that fit into the slots cut for them in the metal-work of the stock, would not, *if well fitted*, entirely obviate any such movements. If these lumps were to break off, all the multitude of 'fancy grips' and top fastenings that could be put to a gun would tear away like so much paper.

No; a good gun does not require these popular but little understood, and generally useless, additions, and is amply strong enough without them; and this I can testify to from the experience of hard shooting for a good many years.

That these projections are greatly in the way an impartial observer can see for himself, especially if he be out shooting when his fingers are cold or wet. Indeed, it is scarcely possible to get a grip with an extractor with some of these top-fastened guns, the breech-end of their barrels being so blocked up with hooks and knobs, and tags and bobs, and what not besides, that only about a quarter of the rim of a cartridge is available to take a pull at. We cannot all afford to purchase ejectors ; and even with the latter the same arguments apply, when it is necessary to withdraw a loaded case, should the gun be fitted with projections of the kind I have alluded to.

The strongest, neatest, and simplest fastening for a gun ever devised is Mr. Purdey's. It is one now utilised by nearly every gunmaker in the kingdom ; and a gun *properly* fitted with his ' snap-bolt action ' will stand as hard work and last as long a time as any gun can do. I have known many guns with the Purdey action, and without any projection on the breech to add to their safety, that have fired 5,000 shots a season for years without a symptom of the shakiness or other necessity for repair which the advocates of the doll's-head and top fastenings declare is sure to take place without these ugly and fanciful incumbrances.

Should a gun without a top fastening require tightening up, it can be cheaply and easily set right ; but if a gun with a top fastening wears loose, it is a troublesome affair to even make it appear tight again. I write 'appear' because, in nine cases out of ten, any such refitting cannot be really done at all, though *at first* it may *seem* that it has been.

STEEL AND DAMASCUS BARRELS

The best material for gun-barrels is an oft-discussed question among sportsmen, more especially in relation to the merits of Damascus and steel. There is only one class of steel that a gunmaker should use in the manufacture of his barrels, and that is the best. Though there are several kinds of steel, of various degrees of excellence, there is none nearly so good as Sir Joseph Whitworth's Fluid Compressed. This is a splendid material in every respect; its powers of endurance and its immense strength are undoubted, and well proved from experience. By reason of its adamantine hardness, and consequent capability of retaining a smooth surface under friction, barrels constructed of this material are less liable to rust and wear than barrels made on any other system I am acquainted with; and certainly, if well bored, no barrels shoot harder or last longer in good condition.

A sportsman will, however, do well to make sure he possesses this excellent steel in his barrels, as there are inferior grades used for inferior guns.[1] I therefore recommend a shooter who prefers steel barrels to procure his gun from a first-class maker whom he can trust, and who has a first-class reputation to keep up; the purchaser may then feel confident that his barrels are really of Whitworth steel, if he is assured by his

---

[1] Whitworth steel is *only* made in one quality—the best; other varieties of steel are, however, manufactured in different grades.

gunmaker that this is the case. Though it is not a common custom, I consider all barrels made of Whitworth's compressed steel should be plainly lettered to that effect, as a guarantee of their make; for this steel certainly has a plain appearance, and, for all the shooter can discover, it might be common metal.

The Whitworth barrels cost some 3*l*. a pair more than the best Damascus; but they are well worth the extra outlay, as they will last with care almost a lifetime, and, to my mind, have the great advantage of retaining their pristine excellence for a longer time under hard use than barrels of any other material. Many gunmakers declare that best steel barrels are stronger than best Damascus, and can, in consequence, be made lighter; and, as some of them carry this theory into practice with success, the surmise is probably a correct one.

There is one point, however, regarding steel barrels, that I must refer to, which is more or less against them. This is, that under rapid firing they certainly heat more quickly than is the case with Damascus; though, on the other hand, they cool in a shorter time —the latter attribute being, however, of no particular advantage. The report caused by steel barrels is also a peculiarity, and, were a shooter to use a couple of guns, one with steel and the other with Damascus barrels, the difference of sound on firing would be very noticeable—so much so, that it would be apt to put him off his shooting; for an occurrence of this kind is always liable to puzzle a shooter, and affect the accuracy of his aim.

If a shooter values the look of his gun—as many sportsmen rightly do—or if he grudges the extra cost of Whitworth steel, then best English Damascus barrels are the most suitable for him to use; for not only are they very handsome, but they carry evident proof of their excellence in their appearance. That best Damascus barrels are, practically speaking, as safe and good as those of fluid compressed steel, is undeniable, though the latter may possess a few small advantages, and are, besides, very fashionable at present. As to the shooting capabilities of Damascus or laminated steel barrels, they cannot be excelled; in fact, in the latter respect, and particularly in regard to regularity of pattern, I find these barrels are sometimes slightly superior to those made of fluid compressed steel.

There is, however, some little uncertainty about our English Damascus. Really good English Damascus barrels, when they *can* be obtained, are superior to Belgian; but those of English make vary considerably in their excellence. They are also produced in much smaller quantities, and are often difficult to obtain just as required. The Belgian Damascus are more regular as to figure, and more free from 'specks' and 'greys,' than are the English, besides being softer, and easier to work. For these reasons many of our gunmakers find it simpler to procure their barrels from

Belgium, as there is a very small percentage of inferior quality imported from that country, and as many as wanted can also be easily procured at short notice. As it is the fashion of English sportsmen to imagine that nothing good in the way of guns or barrels can reach us from the Continent, Belgian Damascus, in order to fall in with this popular delusion, is often sold as English. Still, if a gun is fitted with best Damascus, whether of English or foreign make, it is of small consequence to the shooter; but the fact remains, that so-called English Damascus is frequently Belgian, and that the Belgian barrels of this manufacture are, generally speaking, more reliable than those made in England.

The most ardent supporters of our old friends, the Damascus barrels, have not yet been able to pick a hole in their rivals of fluid compressed steel, save that the latter are supposed to be more liable to fracture under extremes of heat and cold. All I can say is, that I have frequently fired steel barrels until they were too hot to hold, and I have also fired them from a duck-punt during severe frost, when, from frozen water, they were more like lumps of ice than gun-barrels, and I never knew them go wrong. For actual sporting purposes, such tests as these are, in my opinion, ample; though how a barrel will behave after being heated red-hot in a forge, or kept in a refrigerator for a week, I do not know. Nor do I consider its behaviour under such unusual tests would affect the question of its safety in ordinary use, though the blow-up which occurs under some such extraordinary conditions may interest the experimentalist who endeavours to find out how many thousand times more strain a barrel will stand, before it bursts, than could possibly be applied to it by a shooter.

LENGTH OF GUN-BARRELS

I will now say a little about the length of the barrels of a gun. Shortening the barrels without having them re-bored is always a hazardous experiment, as far as their subsequent performance is concerned. In the first place, cutting down the length of the barrels is *certain* to spoil the balance of the gun, whatever be afterwards done in the way of weighting the stock; and it generally causes them to scatter the shot more than they did before the alteration, the result being a larger proportion of weak, divergent, and hence useless, pellets. If a shooter fancies short barrels, they should be made short in the first instance, and bored to suit their length; for if he has his barrels shortened without their being re-bored, he is sure to lessen his chances of killing his game. I have had several barrels cut for experiment $\frac{1}{32}$nd of an inch at a time, in order to test them at the target for pattern and force; and these results have invariably occurred. Personally, I do not believe in barrels under 28 in., even when so constructed on the gun being made, whether the gun in question be a No. 12 or a smaller size. Though I have used and seen used many guns with barrels of about 26 in., I cannot say they were in several respects as successful as those with barrels of 30 in.; the latter length being proved, by long custom and endless experiments on the part of gunmakers and shooters, to be the most suitable to a 12-bore, both in regard to the performance of the gun and its load, and its practical application to a steady and correct aim.

I am, however, ready to admit that I can discover little difference in the actual performances of a gun with 28 in. barrels from a gun with 30 in. barrels; but, once the length is less than 28 in., the pattern and penetrative force suffer. And this falling-off in power is particularly noticeable when a 12-bore gun has barrels of not more than 26 in., though these be most carefully bored and regulated on the gun being made; for they do not shoot nearly so well, especially in regard to pattern, as a gun with 28 in. or 30 in. barrels: and recollect, a long barrel will kill as well at a short distance as a long one, *but* a short barrel will *not* kill well at a long distance.

As to these short barrels being convenient in aiming, this is open to question. If a shooter did nothing but fire at rabbits in covert at short range, he would find them handy enough, there is no doubt; but we do not require a weapon that is convenient for use in one style of shooting and not so in another. At close-lying birds rising before a shooter, a short barrel, whether 25 in. or 20 in. long, would be equally easy to aim with; but let the shooter try a short barrel—one, for example, of 26 in.—at *overhead* or *crossing* birds, and he will soon see its defects. In such shots the barrels seem to swing faster than you wish, and the gun-muzzle to jump and frisk about the sky. I certainly find a short barrel is awkward to align at any but the easiest straightforward birds or at rabbits at close quarters, and that it is particularly difficult to place the muzzle of a short-barrelled gun on fast-driven game. To give a somewhat far-fetched illustration of the advantage of using a gun with a barrel as long as a shooter can *conveniently* use, and as long as is *suitable* to the load of a gun, I will point out that *if* a shooter could wield a gun that almost touched the game he aimed at, he could scarcely miss—hence, the shorter the barrel the less accurate the aim, and the farther from the mark will any deviation of the gun-muzzle cause the charge to travel. Now, as a shooter *cannot* with comfort or manual success handle and aim a gun with *longer* barrels than 28 in. to 30 in., and as *this* length is best adapted to the *shooting* of a 12-bore gun in regard to its charges of powder and shot, its adoption has naturally become general, in preference to a shorter and more unsuccessful length.

A sportsman who has been in the habit of using a gun with the long, swinging, easy balance given by a

30 in. barrel, will at once notice, when *aiming*, the stumpy, unhandy, ill-balanced, tumble-about *feel* of a gun with barrels of several inches less, though the gun itself may weigh lighter in the scale.

Of course, a shooter may become accustomed by constant practice to any length, however short; but if he uses barrels under 28 in. in a 12-bore gun, he will not shoot so successfully at *all-round* game as he would do with barrels of from 28 in. to 30 in. in length. As to placing the muzzle of a short-barrelled gun quicker on flying game than a long barrel, this is an undoubted mistake. What *does* happen, and what leads a shooter into an incorrect supposition, is the power a short gun gives him of putting it up with a quick jerk to his shoulder; but the speed in this case has too much unsteadiness about it, and has a bad effect on the barrels being aligned with accuracy—the latter an attribute of successful aiming that belongs to a 30 in. barrel in a greater degree than to one of several inches less length; for, the shorter the barrels, the more like pointing a pistol does aiming become.

LETTER VI

THE MERITS OF CHOKES AND CYLINDERS, AS APPLIED TO THEIR EFFECT ON GAME AND SUITABILITY TO THE SHOOTER

WE will suppose that a shooter has now found a gun to suit him as regards weight, balance, and mechanism. He has, however, to decide on its boring; and this feature of his gun is the one of all others, next to a perfect fit and a suitable weight, that he will have to consider most: for the question of whether his gun should be bored a choke or a cylinder is a very interesting one to the shooter, and is at all times a subject of *great* importance in regard to his success as a game-shot.

CHOKED BARRELS

I need scarcely explain that a choke, by compressing the charge of shot just before it leaves the muzzle, throws it closer than does a cylinder—the latter having no contraction of the barrels for this purpose. If the shooter decide on a choke, he will also have to determine how much choke his barrels are to contain; that is to say, how many pellets he wishes them to place on the regulation 30 in. in diameter circle at

40 yards. Shooters are apt to look upon all choked barrels as being full-chokes, and capable in the case of 12-bores (to which I here alone allude) of making a pattern of 200. This is a mistake, as a modified choke makes a pattern, for example, of about 150 on the 30 in. circle; and there is *then* little material difference between a gun that acts thus and a cylinder that makes a pattern of some score pellets less.

There is no doubt a choked gun shoots with more force than a cylinder, though only slightly; but I have never found this superiority exist to such an extent as to cause any noticeable effect on game at sporting-ranges, though at the target the full-choke will penetrate at 40 yards a couple more sheets of paper than the cylinder.

What a choke does is this: it carries its charge of shot closer, and so, of course, puts more pellets into the game than can a cylinder; and this attribute at a long distance naturally tells in favour of the choke, provided the aim is sufficiently correct to place its smaller shot-circle on the mark. Up to 35 or 40 yards (the latter being a long shot), a cylinder or a slightly-choked gun is far easier to hit with, and therefore *a more deadly gun to use,* than a full-choke, and either will place amply sufficient pellets in the game to stop it well and neatly without wounding, even at a longer distance. At 35 yards a full-choke will place in the game half as many more pellets than are required to kill, which not only spoils its flesh for the table, but prevents

VI. DISADVANTAGES OF FULL-CHOKED BARRELS

the bird being kept till fit for cooking, from its perforated condition.[1]

I have, over and over again, seen full-chokes and cylinders tried on game with a view to demonstrating the great advantages of the former; and, on my word, I cannot discover that any superiority exists. In the case of ninety-nine out of a hundred shooters I find that the chokes have more disadvantages than the reverse. An average marksman—such as nineteen people out of every twenty are—is certainly handicapped when using a full-choke; for his gun requires more accurate aim than if he were using a cylinder, as it throws its shot in so small a circle; and it stands to reason that, at the distance at which game is *usually* fired at, which is at a far shorter range than many people imagine, it is easier to hit a moving mark with a fairly large circle of shot, covering a good space, than it is to hit it with a small circle covering a small space.

[1] I have seen driven partridges—birds which a shooter is often obliged to fire at within 18 to 20 yards or not at all—so shattered by the mass of shot plastered into them by a full-choke that nine to the dozen were best suited for ferret-meat! Last season, for the sake of experiment, I killed six driven partridges with a full-choke at the ordinary range at which these birds come over a high hedge in a level country, and on reaching home I counted the holes drilled through their skins, which were respectively, 37, 33, 32, 29, 21, 19. The next day I killed six more birds with a cylinder at the same stand, and at the same average distances; result in pellets to birds—17, 15, 12, 12, 9, 7. The latter six birds were brought down as clean as could be wished, and dropped without a flutter. These were, however, *all* fit to *eat*, the previous six being only fit to *drink* in the form of soup.

If a shooter be a *really* first-class shot, he may do wonders with a full-choke, as he will generally strike his mark whether it is near or distant, and he will on occasions bring down his game at very long ranges, when with a cylinder, by reason of its wider-spreading pattern, he might not do so. Yet even a first-class shot, when using a full-choke, has to aim more accurately at game at moderate distances than would be required of him were he using a cylinder; and whether, for the sake of occasional long, brilliant shots, that not seldom entice a man into a habit of random shooting, it is worth while to carry a gun that is not so easy to kill with at an ordinary range, is more than doubtful.

In these days, when driving the game is so much practised, the shooter, good shot though he be, who handles a full-choked gun, is always at a disadvantage, especially in regard to comparatively small birds, such as partridges, and even grouse—birds that generally pass pretty close when driven towards him. It may readily be understood that it is more difficult to hit a bird flying directly towards you with a full-choke gun, that carries its charge of shot concentrated in a space you might almost cover with your hat at twenty paces, than with a gun that has a spread of half as much more, yet puts amply sufficient pellets on the mark to kill, and at the same time shoots practically as hard as any choke-bore.

At driven birds, such as pheasants, grouse or partridges, which are *generally* killed at under 30 yards' distance from the shooter, the cylinder-gun will kill as well as the full-choke, without the drawbacks in regard to the necessity of superior accuracy attending the smaller pattern of the latter. Firing with a full-choke at a driven partridge topping a hedge is almost like discharging a bullet at a cricket-ball whizzing past. Yet, in the hands of the exceptional performer, the choke certainly gives him a remarkable power of *killing*; though in the hands of the average shot it has an equally remarkable power of causing *misses*.

Putting on one side for the present the exceptional marksman, the only real advantages I can discover in favour of a full-choke are:—First, when it is in the hands of a slow shot, who habitually shoots his game over dogs or walks it up before him. In such case the game, in nine cases out of ten, goes directly away from the shooter, and he has often plenty of time to aim almost as with a rifle; and he is, by using a choke, enabled to take a surer and longer sight, as, from the choke carrying its shot fairly close at a long distance, the extra dozen yards the game has run or flown whilst the shooter hesitates over his aim is not of much consequence. Secondly, a full-choke is useful to any one for walking up game if wild, with or without dogs, as, when birds persistently *rise* at about 40 yards, there is no doubt a choke will put more pellets into them than a cylinder, and, of course, succeed in killing them better—as, provided the game is struck—which in *such* shooting is a comparatively *simple* matter—it is as easy to kill it with a choke at 45 to 50 yards as it is with a cylinder at 35 to 40, the pattern of the two guns being very similar in spread at these distances; though, if both are used at shorter and more usual sporting-ranges, the cylinder, whether in the hands of a moderate or a good shot, will be found the more successful weapon of the two.

I have always noticed, when experimenting at the target, that full-choke guns are more variable in their performances than cylinders, and are liable now and then—perhaps once in twenty shots—to shoot patchy, as well as to put the bulk of the shot in a cluster to the right or left; and then, however correct the aim, such irregularity may cause what appears an unaccountable miss at an easy bird. For example, if a full-choke shows, as the result of fifty shots (I never fire less to strike an average), that its pattern is 210, this average will be made up of shots that vary from 240 to as low as 120, with an occasional 100. If the same number of shots are fired from a cylinder or a medium choke, and the average in the former case is 130, and in the latter 150, the extremes will respectively not vary more than—cylinder, 120 *to* 135; medium choke, 135 *to* 160.

There is no doubt that, even in the hands of the fairly good shot, a cylinder is the most killing gun to use for all-round shooting at ordinary game at sporting-ranges; and a full-choked gun is the most unsuitable weapon for this purpose, and particularly so in regard to *all* driven birds.

A good shot may use a gun of modified choke that places 150 to 160 pellets on the 30 in. circle at 40 yards, and do well with it; but I do not believe there are five men in England who can drop their game, both driven and springing, as satisfactorily with a full-choke as they can with a cylinder or medium-choke; though, in the hands of the two or three who *can* do so, a full-choke is the most effective gun they can use. But then such first-class marksmen as I have in my mind would almost kill their game with a rifle-bullet, so accurate is their aim. To such shooters as *these* a close or well-spread pattern is a matter of small moment at a short range (though the close pattern will surely disgust the epicure and his cook), and at a long one the former is *to them* the most effective.

CYLINDER BARRELS

It is an error to imagine that long shots cannot be killed with a cylinder-gun. I have often seen cylinders kill at as long a distance as any choke.

It may be said that a good cylinder, throwing a regularly-spread pattern of 130 to 135, will kill almost every time, if held straight, up to 40 yards; and that is a *long* distance if paced in the open, and farther than one in a thousand rocketing pheasants pass overhead.

En passant I will remark there is no commoner mistake made among shooters than the height of rocketing pheasants. When these birds are seen to fly at an unusual altitude, they are imagined to be in the clouds; and I have often heard on such occasions the exclamation, after a miss, 'That bird must have been quite 50 yards up; I couldn't touch him.'

A pheasant 150 ft. above ground would appear so small and far that few shooters of experience would fire at him at all, especially if lower birds were on the wing or expected.

If you see an overhead pheasant against the open sky at, we will say, only 105ft., he will seem almost any height—40 yards in your imagination at least; but supposing this wonderfully high bird passes by or just over a tall tree, you will be surprised how much lower his distance above ground really is, and how much nearer to the top of the tree his flight takes him than you could have fancied possible. I have but taken a pheasant at 35 yards high as an example. A bird flying at an elevation nearly half as high again, as they are often *said* to attain, would indeed be a 'teazer' to tumble down!

The height good sporting pheasants fly when driven overhead (unless, of course, the shooter is posted in a deep valley) may be set down at 25 yards to 30 yards, high birds at 30 yards to 35 yards, and exceptionally tall ones at 35 yards to 40 yards; the latter height being very rarely attained.

From this we can easily realise how it is a cylinder *should* bring down 'rocketers' at any reasonable height, and how such birds are well within its reach, though people may consider a full-choke would alone be effective at the longer ranges. It is curious that though a pheasant flying low appears within easy range at 30 yards, yet the same bird travelling 30 yards above ground seems so much more distant as a perpendicular shot.

I have seen shooters—good shots, too—purposely armed with full-chokes, blazing away at rocketing pheasants said to be too high for cylinders, and have heard them say on missing, 'That bird was too high for even my full-choke'; and I have on the same occasion seen a man, certainly a first-class shot, stand well behind and pull down bird after bird as dead as need be, after they had been feathered by the guns in front, his gun being nothing but an ordinary cylinder making a pattern, as I afterwards tested myself, of 130 at 40 yards!

I am aware these remarks concerning cylinders and chokes will rouse the ire of those few gunmakers who are still behind the age concerning the *practical* uses of a gun *in the field*, and who advertise and recommend a full-choke as perfection for everybody; but then, they take their arguments from the target, which is in *this* case a decidedly unreliable mentor.

An enthusiast on chokes will tell you that cylinder 12-bores which put 130 pellets or so on a round target of 30 in. diameter at 40 yards are quite useless for killing game with certainty at over 35 yards. They will also impress upon you that cylinder barrels which are capable of placing 130 pellets on the 30 in. circle are not cylinders at all, but are in reality barrels with a slight amount of choke in them. This is certainly an incorrect idea. It is true that what is termed a cylinder-gun may *not* be a cylinder pure and simple; but, on the other hand, it may not have a vestige of choke about it. However, to appease these sceptics, let us suppose a so-called cylinder *has* an infinitesimal tightening towards the muzzle, or recess choke in its barrel, and makes in consequence a pattern of 130 to 135—it is this pattern, I maintain, that will kill, and, for the ordinary marksman to use on all-round game, is best adapted to kill, whatever the boring of the gun be, if the shot is regularly spread over the target. The advocates of chokes declare that a pattern of even 140 is too low a one for the shooter to kill well with, save at a very moderate range.

I have seen many cylinder-guns make a pattern of 130 to 135 with great regularity; guns without a symptom of choke in their boring—rather the reverse, as can easily be ascertained by the use of a gunmaker's gauge.

The fact is, really good cylinder barrels are difficult to make, and, to get them up to a high standard of shooting, they require most careful boring. On the other hand, a choked barrel is simplicity itself in comparison, and can easily be regulated to bunch its shot up to the target in a thick cluster.

A cheap cylinder-gun that will constantly make a regular pattern of even 120 on the 30 in. circle at 40 yards is a *rara avis*; but a cheap gun can be choked to place 180 to 200 pellets with ease, as the latter attainment requires far less care and expense to produce. And the dealer in inferior guns will generally avoid, if he possibly can, selling a cylinder-gun, especially to a shooter who wishes to see its performance at a target before purchase. The would-be buyer will usually be told: 'Don't have a cylinder, sir; all good shots use chokes now, as they kill much farther.'

LETTER VII

THE MERITS OF CHOKES AND CYLINDERS
(continued)

SOME of the advice given to shooters in the choice of guns is very laughable. For example, Mr. Greener writes in a recent book: 'The cylinder-gun must not be used at distances greater than 30 yards; to do so is unnecessarily cruel.' Dear me! If he could only see grouse and pheasants, and other game, killed stone-dead by a good shot time after time with a cylinder at over 40 yards, as I often and often have seen, how he would stare, to be sure! He would probably say: 'Well, if a cylinder-gun does kill so well, it ought not to.' But that goes for nothing. It is what a cylinder-gun *can* do—and what I and many other shooters are ready to vouch it *will* do, if properly used—that gives weight to the argument; for an ounce of proof is worth a ton of fancy.

For my part, I have killed hundreds and hundreds of tough-plumaged birds, such as wild duck, and wild geese, too, at 40 yards and more, with an old cylinder 12-bore 'cripple-stopper' by 'Reilly' that in its best days could not put more than 120 pellets on the 30in.

VII. THE ADVANTAGES OF CYLINDER BARRELS 79

circle at 40 yards, with 304 pellets of No. 6—the charge I used, moreover, being 1½oz. of No. 5 shot.

Mr. Greener also writes that he thinks especially badly of cylinders, because when he tried one at a stationary pigeon at 35 yards he failed to kill it. What sportsman does not know how difficult it is to kill with certainty a wounded bird running or squatting on the ground, whether with a cylinder or a choke, at even a less distance, merely because the bird's body is protected as with armour by its closed wings?

I will, therefore, say to the young shooter: If your aim is fairly true, you can, with a cylinder-gun, kill your game at any range at which it should be fired at,[1] and, taking all-round shooting into consideration,

[1] How far is this? Well, I should say no game-birds ought, as a rule, to be fired at with a cylinder or medium choke beyond 45 yards, or ground game at over 40 yards. Of course, a large bird like a pheasant, that offers a good-sized target, *may* sometimes with a full-choke be killed clean at 55 yards, *if* a crossing shot; but it is far more likely to be wounded. Partridges and grouse, however, being smaller birds, will not receive so many pellets at 55 yards as a pheasant does; and though they might be struck every time, yet they likely enough would not drop dead once to half a dozen hits, even with a full-choke. Fifty yards is a long distance at which to drop birds *dead* with any certainty; and it is dead, never wounded game, a true sportsman tries to bring down. People who talk of killing their game *regularly* at 60 to 70 yards, simply talk nonsense. I have never seen the man or gun that could do this. The 70-yard shooter should test his gun for *penetration* at this range, and note the result; for, even should his gun be a full-choke, and make a fair pattern on the target at 60 to 70 yards, yet this is no proof whatever that it will *kill* at these distances, though it may pepper the game all over. The pattern of a gun is very misleading at a long range—at 65

very much better than you will with a full-choke, for reasons I have tried to explain. And if your aim be *not* true, the choke will certainly not help you to kill, on account of its small shot-circle; whilst, on the other hand, a cylinder, by reason of its larger pattern covering more space, allows for some inaccuracy of aim, and hence, without doubt, will be of assistance in filling the bag, particularly in the case of *all* driven game.[1]

A cylinder 12-bore gun should, if it is properly bored, place 130 pellets of shot on the 30 in. circle at 40 yards with a charge of 1½oz. of No. 6 shot, containing 304 pellets, or 270 to the ounce. A full-choke should place 200 to 220, and a modified choke 150 to 160: and it should be borne in mind that a constant regularity of pattern, and even distribution

---

yards, for instance—as in reality only a part of the shot-charge then reaches a moving mark; the remainder—quite one-third at 65 yards—straggles weakly up, probably after the bird aimed at is out of the line of fire. In the case, however, of a stationary target, *all* the charge is shown thereon, as if it arrived simultaneously, and the shooter is too ready to accept this non-reliable pattern as evidence of what a number of pellets his gun can place on game at 60 to 70 yards. It is the shots *under* 40 yards that add up the bag. Let me see a man kill these regularly and neatly, and I do not care what he does *over* 40 yards; for the latter are the exception, and the former the rule!

[1] Lord de Grey uses a full-choke, and Lord Walsingham a gun without *any* choke; yet both these gentlemen kill their game in brilliant style, near or far. At the same time, this is no proof that the average marksman would drop *his* game with a full-choke as well as he would with a cylinder; though it does show him what he *might* do with a cylinder *if* he had the gift of using it with sufficient accuracy.

of the shot *all over* the 30 in. circle, is a *sine quâ non* in the shooting of a good gun.

It is a sign of a badly-bored gun when it places a high pattern on the target at one shot and a low one at another; and the gun is equally faulty if it places a thick cluster of shot on one part of the target, though this cluster be in the very centre, and spreads the pellets thinly over the rest of it; for it is a mere chance if the shooter places the thick cluster of pellets on his mark. And I may point out, that when the pellets are close together in one part of the shot-circle, they are proportionately scattered, and hence more or less useless, in another part.

If a shooter is a fairly good shot—a man, for instance, who, at ordinary ranges, and firing only *one* barrel, can pretty regularly kill seven out of ten partridges rising before him, and perhaps five out of seven pheasants passing overhead at a fair height and pace, and say three out of five driven grouse— then he may, if he fancies his shooting will be improved thereby, use a modified choke making a pattern of 150 on the 30 in. circle at 40 yards. Should he find that, with the latter gun, he kills near shots as well as he did before making a change, he will be a decided gainer in the matter of long shots; but should he advance another step, and take to a full-choke, he will surely notice that, though he is still successful at the long shots, the ones at ordinary distances will be not seldom missed!

It is worth remark, that though the appliances for boring cylinder barrels are just the same as eighty years ago, yet, owing to the immensely-increased popularity of shooting since the advent of breech-loaders, the boring of these barrels, from the additional care bestowed on their construction, has vastly improved during recent years; for instance, a cylinder of thirty years ago was a rare good gun if it made a pattern of 100—96 to 98 being the usual thing in those days, and previously. The present improvement in the shooting of cylinder-guns has often been attributed to their containing a certain amount of choke in their boring—a supposition that may be correct in some cases, but not generally, and especially not in the case of first-class guns.

A 12-bore gun that will *regularly* and *evenly* place 130 pellets on the 30 in. circle at 40 yards is a first-rate game-gun in every way for the average marksman; and I will say the *perfect* gun for general shooting, and the use of a good shot, is the one that will just cover a space representing a 30 in. circle at 20 yards—of course, killing anything in that space, and by such a spread giving the shooter a good chance of hitting his mark (as in the case of small, driven birds, such as partridges)—and will put enough pellets into a 36 in. circle at 35 yards to kill well within *that* space at *this* distance. This a modified choke with a pattern of 150 at 40 yards on the 30 in. circle should do. On the other hand, a full-choke at 20 yards only covers about half a 30 in. circle, and at 35 yards, though it places more pellets in the 30 in. circle than the cylinder, it puts more than sufficient, the cylinder or the medium choke putting in plenty to kill; and more than that we do not want. Again, if the aim be somewhat incorrect, the pellets outside the 30 in. circle, in the case of the cylinder or modified choke, assist the shooter; while, in the case of the full-choke, there is little assistance of the kind, as very few of its pellets go outside the circle, even at 40 yards. As an example, it can be taken that, in the case of a shooter firing at a driven partridge at 20 yards, he may consider he fires with a cylinder a circle of shot nearly 30 in. wide; with a choke his circle is only 18 in. across!

In connection with this letter I append some reduced patterns (scale, $\frac{1}{30}$ in. = 1 in.), which are useful in showing the effect on game of cylinder and full-choked guns at different distances, and which are the average result of many hundred shots fired by me at full-sized outlines cut in paper and pasted on the 30 in. target.

In the case represented by Fig. 1, the shooter would have killed his bird had it been, instead, in the position of one of the outside birds shown, or 15in. from the sight he took—*i.e.* the centre of the shot-circle.

In Fig. 2, the shooter would kill his bird three times over, and riddle it with shot, *if* he hits it at all! If, however, the shooter had aimed 10 in. to one side or other, he might have clean missed his bird, or only winged it, when, with a cylinder-gun, he would have

FIG. 1.—CYLINDER-GUN AT A DRIVEN PARTRIDGE
(distance, 20 yards).

Partridges (and circle representing 30 in. in diameter) $\frac{1}{10}$th full size. 260 pellets inside 30 in. circle, and spread all over it; 40 pellets outside 30 in. circle, within a breadth of 9 in.

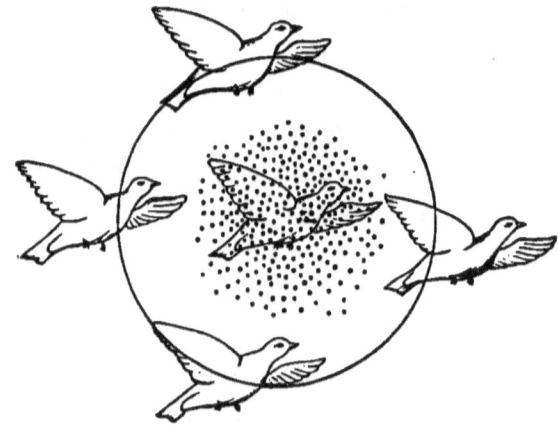

FIG. 2.—FULL-CHOKED GUN AT A DRIVEN PARTRIDGE
(distance, 20 yards).

Partridges (and circle representing 30 in. in diameter) $\frac{1}{10}$th full size. All the charge of shot (304 pellets No. 6 = 1¼ oz.) in the centre of the 30 in. circle.

scored a kill (*vide* Fig. 1). It will also be seen, had

he shot at one of the outside birds, how near to the mark his aim might have been taken without his striking it.

In Fig. 3 we again have a shot-pattern that allows some 15 in. for inaccurate aim, as, had the pheasant been that distance from its position below, or the sight taken by the shooter, as represented by the

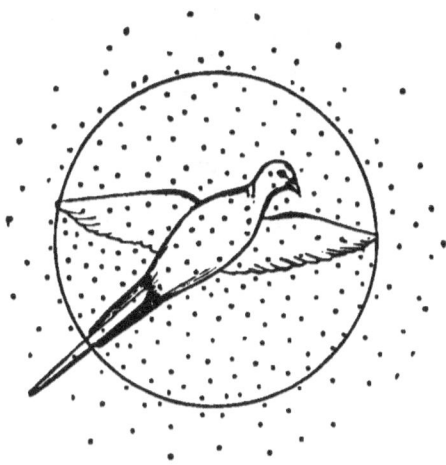

FIG. 3.—CYLINDER-GUN AT A PHEASANT
(distance, 30 yards).

Pheasant (and circle representing 30 in. in diameter) ₁/₇th full size. 174 pellets inside 30 in. circle; 86 pellets outside 30 in. circle, within a breadth of 9 in.

centre of the shot-circle, it would have equally been killed.

In the case of Fig. 4, the shooter will have to place all his charge of shot right smack on his bird, or he will probably wound it, as there are no pellets outside the actual width of the object itself to assist in case of an inaccurate aim.

86 LETTERS TO YOUNG SHOOTERS LETTER

A pheasant at 40 yards, crossing low, is a good long shot; a pheasant flying overhead at 40 yards is

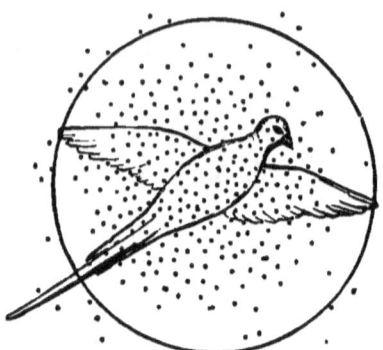

FIG. 4.—FULL-CHOKED GUN AT A PHEASANT
(distance, 30 yards).

Pheasant (and circle representing 30 in. in diameter) $\frac{1}{15}$th full size. 274 pellets inside 30 in. circle (sufficient to spoil, and many more than enough to kill); 21 pellets outside 30 in. circle, within a breadth of 9 in.

FIG. 5.—CYLINDER-GUN AT A PHEASANT
(distance, 40 yards).

Pheasant (and circle representing 30 in. in diameter) $\frac{1}{10}$th full size. 133 pellets in the 30 in. circle; 100 pellets outside 30 in. circle, within a breadth of 9 in.

rarely seen: yet, from the example shown in Fig. 5, we can realise that a gun placing 130 to 135 pellets on the 30 in. circle at 40 yards should at the latter distance make a live bird into a dead one. In this case it will be seen that the pheasant would have been killed had it been 15 in. in any direction from the shooter's aim, as represented by the centre of the shot-circle, as there are a very useful number of pellets outside the 30 in. circle to assist him. A full-choked gun would place 220 to 230 pellets inside the 30 in. circle at 40 yards, and about 60 to 70 outside, within a radius of 9 in. The choked gun would, of course, put more lead into the body of the pheasant —more, in fact, than required to kill—the cylinder, however, putting plenty for this purpose. The latter gun gives 100 pellets, well spread, just outside the 30 in. circle to assist the shooter; the choke would give but 60 to 70, irregularly placed, from their number being less.

In Fig. 6, of course, the pattern is thin; still it is one that, in the case of a gun with good penetration, might bring down the bird, though not often, as a dead one, for at 50 yards the shot-charge from *any* gun strikes with *very* much less force than it does at even 40 yards.

In Fig. 7 we have a first-class killing pattern, and which, at the long range of 50 yards, closely resembles the pattern of a cylinder-gun at 35 yards, or a medium choke at 40 yards. But then, nineteen out of

Fig. 6.—CYLINDER-GUN AT A PHEASANT
(distance, 50 yards).

Pheasant (and circle representing 30 in. in diameter) $\frac{1}{10}$th full size. 78 pellets inside 30 in. circle; 90 pellets outside 30 in. circle, within a breadth of 9 in.

Fig. 7.—FULL-CHOKED GUN AT A PHEASANT
(distance, 50 yards).

Pheasant (and circle representing 30 in. in diameter) $\frac{1}{10}$th full size. 156 pellets inside 30 in. circle; 104 pellets outside 30 in. circle, within a breadth of 9 in.

twenty birds offer shots at from 25 to 30 yards, and few are killed at 35 to 40 yards. As to ground game, *their* distance is generally nearer 20 yards than 30. If birds or ground game habitually gave chances at 45 to 50 yards, *then* this pattern of the full-choked gun would be invaluable, though at usual ranges the cylinder-gun would be much easier to hit with, the pattern of the latter being in such case more than half as large again as that of the full-choke. How-

FIG. 8.—FULL-CHOKED GUN AT A RABBIT CROSSING
(distance, 25 yards).
The aim is too forward, and the rabbit missed by a few inches only.

ever, even with the pattern shown in Fig. 7, to make certain of *killing* his bird the shooter will have to place the 30 in. shot-circle pretty fair on the mark, as within the 9 in. radius outside this circle the pellets are thinly scattered, and scarcely exceed in number the pellets thrown by the cylinder-gun at the same distance. One of the reasons why game is so often wounded with a full-choke is because a shooter is so apt to place the fringe of the pattern on the mark, instead of the closest cluster of the shot, as performing the *latter* feat naturally requires an *exact* aim on his part!

The two examples represented in Figs. 8 and 9 (scale, $\frac{1}{20}$th full size) show how a cylinder assists a shooter at an ordinary range, whether at ground game

FIG. 9.—CYLINDER-GUN AT A RABBIT CROSSING
(distance, 25 yards).
The aim taken at the same spot as in Fig. 8, and also too forward; yet, owing to the wider spread of the shot, the rabbit is killed.

or birds, and how a full-choked gun has a contrary effect, from the accurate aim it requires. Had the shooter aimed a similar distance *behind* the rabbit, it would have been wounded by the choke, though killed by the cylinder.

LETTER VIII

HOW TO SHOOT SAFELY, WITH REMARKS ON LOADERS, AND THE SAFE HANDLING OF A GUN IN THE FIELD [1]

I DO not propose to lay down a dozen or more rules concerning how to use a gun safely, as such would be quite unnecessary; for using a gun safely merely means that it should never be handled in a careless manner, either in regard to its mechanism or, above all, the direction of its muzzle.

The only living thing that should be in danger from the gun is the game the shooter wishes to kill; and, whether a gun is at full-cock or half-cock, or has this or that safety bolt, it is equally safe in the hands of a careful man—one with whom, for the sake of illustration, did the gun fire accidentally *a score times a day*, it would injure *nothing* but the earth or —the moon.

It is not, however, from the mere handling of a

---

[1] I wish to point out that to shoot *safely*, and to shoot in a *sportsmanlike manner*, are, in my opinion, attributes of more real importance to a young shooter (and especially to his friends) than are his powers of accuracy ! I shall, therefore, give these two letters priority.

gun, nor yet from wanton stupidity and recklessness, such as crawling through a hedge with the muzzle directed at somebody's back in front, or pointing a gun in joke (save the mark!) or firing it accidentally, that serious accidents are wont to occur, unless with downright idiots, who should shoot together (with a view to their extermination), or not at all. It is more frequently the case that an eye is put out or an injury done in the excitement of shooting; and oftener than not, when an accident does occur, it is caused by the shooter, in his *anxiety to kill the game*, omitting to notice the presence of his companions and their exact positions. It is curious, when a man does pepper you, how apparently astonished he is at the incident, and how he invariably remarks, he cannot for the life of him understand how such a remarkable accident occurred, as he is so particularly careful with his gun at all times!

If a gun, loaded or unloaded, is never pointed dangerously at or near any person, or where any person *might* be, no one can suffer injury.

You ask, how can an unloaded gun do harm, even if pointed at man or dog? It can do great harm, as a man cannot acquire two systems of safety with a gun. If he points it dangerously when unloaded, he will act in a similar way when it is loaded, from mere force of habit. To see guns handled and snapped in a gunmaker's shop as they often are, will cause a careful sportsman to pop out into the street as quickly as he can—at least, that is the effect on myself.

Invariably treat a gun as if loaded and full-cocked, and then, if some foolish fellow carelessly hands you one as though uncharged, when in reality loaded, it is equally safe in your hands, whether you are alone or in a crowd.

There is always plenty of time for a shooter to consider if *every* shot he fires is an absolutely safe one, or the reverse. He can realise this instinctively, without his caution in the least interfering with the accuracy or rapidity of his aim, as it should be an unfailing habit for a shooter, when placed in position for driven birds, or for walking in line, to at once take a general view of his surroundings, and make up his mind where he may fire, and where he had better not; he is then ready for the game, when it appears or rises, in regard to the safety of every shot.

I have heard a shooter remark, in apologetic tones, after showering shot about the head of another sportsman: 'My dear sir, I *am* so sorry; but I could not see you, and had no idea you were behind that hedge; and, though I did not feel quite sure at first whether I was acting safely, the birds were breaking out so fast that I was obliged to fire at them as hard as I could, and really had not time to think of anything else.'

A somewhat plausible excuse on the face of it,

but it embraces in its area the whole question and risk of dangerous aiming.

It is a golden rule never to fire unless you can plainly see *how far the shot is likely to reach*. How far this is few sportsmen are aware. I have known a man's eye seriously damaged at 160 yards—a distance that was carefully measured at the time the accident occurred. If you fire high—I mean almost perpendicularly, as at a pheasant flying overhead—it is all safe, as dropping shot can then do no harm; but to fire at a bird flying low, whether over a young plantation or in a covert, *may* at any time be a very dangerous shot, though quite unintentionally so. Of course, there *might* be no risk; but, by reason of the former possibility, such shots should never, save under exceptional circumstances—as when a line of shooters are walking out a covert with no guns posted forward—be indulged in; and even in the latter case, a beater placed as a 'stop' might easily be brought to bag. In the open country—as when partridge or grouse shooting—it is, of course, another matter.

In rabbit shooting I have noticed more dangerous shots fired than at any kind of game, especially when the ground is undulating. A rabbit careering along the top of a ridge can often be killed neatly and to the satisfaction of the shooter, though perchance the man out of sight in the hollow at the other side of the ridge, coming up with the luncheon or spare cartridges, may have reason to be less pleased.

A really dangerous man at rabbits is the one who prides himself on 'snap-shooting,' and says, 'I fire at the least move in a bush'; and bang goes his gun, whether his shot results in the death of a fine fox, a dog, a pheasant on the ground, or the peppering of a keeper's legs.

I am now alluding only to shooting in covert. Rabbit-shooting in the open, or at birds on the wing, also in the open, and when driven forward, should be safe enough under all circumstances if a good line be kept, and the shooters are in full view of one another. If this is *not* the case, and a tall hedge chance to divide the line, notice should be given when birds are being picked up on one side of the hedge, or the guns on the other side may walk forward and run risks in consequence.

Shooting rabbits in thick covert, or amid brambles, young trees, gorse, or bracken, requires no little circumspection when men and dogs, and other guns besides the young shooter, are to right and left of him, and sometimes behind him. Shooting back cannot be too strictly forbidden on such occasions, for beaters will at times drop out of the line for *various reasons*, as well as hang back, both from fatigue and idleness; and it is a habit of boys, and even men, to throw themselves flat on a wounded rabbit to hold it, as well as to chase, stick in hand, even an unwounded one for a few yards with the foolish idea of its capture. They are then, perhaps, for the moment, concealed from the shooter. Never shall I forget the piteous shrieks of pain, combined with shocking language, emitted by a fat French cook who, for the first time in his life, had come out to see 'le sport,' and who, lagging in the rear, was shot 'too much behind' as he lay in the fern, face downwards, over a burrow, trying to extract therefrom a wounded rabbit with a 'fork.'

Few people are aware to what an extent chance pellets of shot will sometimes diverge or ricochet at 40 yards, even from a 'choke' bore. I have known a sportsman kill a rabbit at this distance in a grass field half-way between two beaters who were quite 30 yards apart, and yet he succeeded in peppering both men; and though I should not have fired the shot myself, I must confess it looked fairly safe to do so.

It is always risky, under any circumstances, to fire back in covert, unless you can see that, without a shadow of a doubt, all is clear and safe on every side; and in covert *this* is rather a difficult thing to prove on the instant. Firing back in thick covert, or even in fairly thick covert, is most reprehensible; and firing through or straight at a hedge is, perhaps, the most dangerous act a shooter can perform. If you injure anybody on such occasions, it is not the smallest excuse apologising on the score you did not or could not see him, as you had no earthly right to fire in the direction a person *might* by some unusual chance happen to be, though unseen by you; nor is it any excuse, after peppering people, explaining to them they had no right to be where they were, as they were out of, or had left, their proper position, as the fact of another person committing an error scarcely palliates a shooter's negligence in wounding him.

Even on some fairly well-organised shooting-days I have seen many risks run, especially if the placing of the guns is left to the judgment of the keepers; for it is the primary object of these gentry to make a bag and show a good list of killed, rather than to give the game a chance. With this end in view, a fearful and not unusual custom of theirs is to drive out a covert in short beats, with one line of guns standing forward, and another line marching up to the first line; the ground game is finally hemmed in between the guns, and, in the case of novices, both lines blaze towards one another.

I have even seen this arrangement still further complicated in its audacious risk by leaving guns back, and a gun to walk forward on either side. But on that day I did *not* feel well, and left for home, though I was interested to learn afterwards that three or four people were the worse for the fray.

There are in the case of some shooters habits of carelessness that seem incurable, though it is charitable to suppose they *do* try to mend their ways. That dreadful one of swinging a gun on game, when such aiming crosses dangerous points, is one of the worst vices of a careless shooter, and has caused many sad accidents. It is a habit that is especially dangerous when birds that fly somewhat low, such as grouse or partridges, are being driven towards the guns. For a shooter to swing his gun on a bird from his front to his rear (finger against trigger, in all probability), crossing with the muzzle, in doing so, other guns within range of his shot—I would almost say within sight of him—is unpardonable, as it is just as easy for him, when wishing to fire behind, to lift the muzzle of his gun well over the line of his friends' heads, afterwards dropping it on to the bird he wishes to kill, so as to clear his companions, and ensure their safety from accident.

The very nervous shooter is almost as dangerous as the very careless one, as the former never seems able to make up his mind, and is as likely at any moment to fire a dangerous shot as a safe one. This class of shooter should be placed at a distance from his friends, and given at the same time careful instructions in which direction he alone may fire, and as little discrimination allowed him as possible in the use of his gun.

Though, let us hope, a careful shot yourself, invariably keep a sharp eye on fellow-sportsmen, and you will soon discover, and hence learn to give a wide berth to, those among your friends who flourish their guns about like a gardener sprinkling his flowers from a watering-pot, or who, so long as they can bang off at any game that rises near or far, will do so, even in the case of doubtfully safe shots. If you cannot retain a safe distance from such shooters as the above, my advice is, go home to write important letters, for 'twere better to run the risk of giving offence than be liable to have your eyesight damaged, or even to be made a sieve of.

If you chance to be shooting for the first time with a stranger, keep on his right-hand side, as it is the usual practice—indeed, natural habit—to carry guns pointing towards the left ; also, force on your companion the compliment of preceding you, even through the most prickly hedge; and recollect when shooting with a farmer—and it is not unusual in these days to propitiate tenants by doing so¹— that if you place yourself so that rabbits are liable to run between you

¹ It is certainly wise policy, as well as kind behaviour, to bestow on tenants such a well-deserved—I may say, well-*earned*—compliment as a day's sport. On large estates it is becoming, I am glad to say, an annual institution that those tenants who are fond of their gun should enjoy a day or two's rabbit-shooting, with a few cock pheasants included, for the benefit of the lucky holders of game licences. I am sure such a day, with its good-fellowship, amply-provided refreshment and equal division of the spoil, is considered not only a genuine treat, but also some small return to the tenants, as the latter generally contribute not a little to the sport experienced by the owner or lessee of the land, by assisting his keepers in the preservation of the game. If a little more generosity of this nature were the fashion, when feasible, we should not hear such complaints as : ' My dear sir, I give you my word, when I went over my shooting the other day there was a farmer with a double-barrelled gun in one hand and a Radical newspaper in the other looking out of every house-door I passed.'

and him, he, honest fellow, will consider killing, or, at all events, firing at the rabbits, the first consideration, and hitting you the second.

LOADERS

Should you be enjoying such good shooting as to require a pair of guns in use at the same time, of all things avoid taking out a loader who is unversed in the handling of a gun; 'twere better to leave him at home to brush your clothes or clean your boots, and be content yourself with less sport.

To see an awkward squad of loaders, footmen, valets, and under-keepers, as one sometimes does, carrying their masters' guns in all positions, and at all angles of danger, both to themselves and every living thing near them, is perfectly appalling; so give your loader some careful drill before you venture to accept his services at your side with a gun.

Teach him to stand on your right side, a little in the rear; to take the fired gun from your right hand into his left as you hold it, muzzle pointing skyward, and hand you the loaded gun from his right into your left hand, muzzle also directed to the stars; and, above all things, make sure that, while in the act of loading, your man never points a gun at anything, except the ground immediately to his right front; and that, on closing the gun, he without fail hinges the stock *up* to the barrels, instead of the barrels to the stock—the former being the *only* safe method for a loader to practise, as he cannot then, by lifting the barrels, cause risk to your companions or yourself should the gun by chance explode. You should also be careful to teach him that, in the movement of raising the gun to hand it to you ready to fire, he should sweep the muzzle clear of all dangerous points.

If you have only fired one barrel, be sure that you put your gun to 'safe' if a hammerless, or let the hammer of the unfired barrel down in the case of a hammer-gun, *before* handing your weapon to be loaded. Do not omit this precaution on any account. Above all things, never permit your loader to touch the hammers or safety-bolt of your gun on handing it to him—*that* is a *sine quâ non*; then, if you follow the above instructions, he cannot possibly fire it, or give it back to you in a dangerous condition.

Do not hurry and flurry your loader by entreating him to load quicker, and so, perhaps, cause him in his anxiety to become careless of previous cautions as to the safe handling of your gun. It is of no use saying to him, 'Hang it, man, look sharp! Here's another bird coming!' If he is not blind, he probably sees it as well as you, and is, may be, grinding his teeth and skinning his fingers over a tight cartridge, or at all events doing all he can as rapidly as he is able. It is well, when using two guns, to carry a half-dozen cartridges in your pocket for emergencies, as by their assistance, just when most required, you may down two or three birds whilst your man is wrestling with and swearing at an obstinate fired case that he cannot extract from your second gun. An extractor dangling from a button by a thong of leather (the latter at least 8in. long, and tucked into an outside pocket) will be found very convenient for occasions such as the above; and let your loader be similarly equipped.

An invariable rule, that should *never* be broken, is for a shooter to extract loaded cartridges from his gun when crossing a stile, a hedge, or a ditch. He should act thus even in the case of an obstruction he can almost step over. Out with the cartridges; doing so and reloading is but the work of a second, gives no trouble, and makes your gun *absolutely* safe; and then, when you *do* catch your foot and fall—though such an accident may but occur once in several seasons—there is no danger of your gun firing from the tumble you give it, and perchance causing an accident you can never forget or cease lamenting.

However securely a loaded gun be held, and however good and reliable its action and safety arrangements, yet a sprawling fall on the shooter's part *might* disarrange its mechanism; and, though the gun chance to fire accidentally but once in your lifetime, that once may, as I have said, do damage beyond all repair. Hence, make it a rule to unload when crossing obstacles, and you cannot inflict harm on yourself or others. By not unloading there is *always* a bare possibility of an accident; and, *however slight* such a chance may be, it is surely better to have *none at all* when you can so easily put all vestige of risk to one side.

Let a hundred shots be lost at birds that rise just as you are scrambling to your feet on the far side of a hedge, rather than cross it with a loaded gun, is my advice.

Be most careful, also, to see that your *loader*, if you happen to be using a pair of guns, pays as much attention to safety on all occasions as you do *yourself*.

If the loader, who has care of your second gun, is a stranger to you, keep a very strict watch on him till you are confident he is an expert; and if he shows by his behaviour he is not, do not allow him to load at all—only to unload, and then merely return the gun ready for *you* to charge from your pocket as required.

Sometimes a shooter cannot bring a loader with him to a shooting party, and is then obliged to borrow one from his host. Never shall I forget the face of a particularly cautious old gentleman who, through some mischance, had been forced to take a strange assistant for the day to bear his second gun. As the sportsman was cautiously climbing a stiff fence and balancing on the top, he inclined a little backwards. His loader, instead of using his hand, propped his temporary master forward with the muzzle of the gun he carried; and, in reply to an angry expostulation, remarked: 'It's all right, sir: the gun is only at half-cock, and I feared you were going to fall.'

While alluding to the subject of loaders, it is worthy of note that the most dangerous position which a shooter can be in is with an untrained assistant in a grouse-box—especially in a circular one. The loader should, in such case, stoop on the right side of the shooter, with the muzzles of the guns, as he charges them, pointed to his front; and he will have to hand you your guns with his left hand—or, better still, stand them ready for you to take up as required. If he loads with the guns pointing inside the box—as he must do in the case of a circular one—he will, unless well looked after, not only be liable to sweep your legs with their muzzles now and again, but will also be very likely to choke the ends of the barrels with turf, for want of space. As a matter of safety and convenience, when a loader is required on the moors, and the shooter has to shift his position for driven birds, there is no double grouse-box so safe as one the ground-plan of which is like the letter H, as here shown. Your loader can in this one half-kneel at your right side, a little behind you, and charge the guns with their muzzles directed towards the open moor; he cannot then blow off your feet, and leave you to 'shoot upon your stumps' for the rest of your life. But the above subject, as well as how to protect the shooters from each other and the best form of boxes, I shall, if I publish another volume, include in a 'Letter on Grouse Driving.'

HOW TO CARRY A GUN SAFELY

I must not omit a few words concerning how to carry a gun with safety. If you are placed on the right flank of other shooters, be very careful, especially when walking in line, not to cover your neighbours on the left with the muzzle of your gun. Though an inexcusable habit, it is one I not seldom witness at intervals towards the end of a long day's sport when the shooters are tired. Of course, if made a regular custom of, the careless shooter who thus acted would be remonstrated with, and rightly, by some one who objected to look up his gun-barrels.

The pleasantest way of carrying a gun, when not expecting many or sudden chances, or when walking from place to place, is doubtless to carry it over the shoulder, the top rib upwards; but the *safest* method is to carry it on your shoulder, top-rib downwards. By adopting the *former* position for the gun, especially if the shooter be of short stature or uneven ground be traversed, the muzzle will now and again point quite low, and therefore dangerously, though the owner of the gun may not be aware of the fact; by the *latter* plan, the gun can only point at the weather-cocks in the neighbourhood.

When walking in line at a good pace and expecting game to rise now and again, carry a gun either under the right arm, muzzle directed straight to the front,[1] or else with the gun athwart your body, the muzzle pointing high across the left breast and well forward—the latter being the readier attitude of the two for a shot.

If walking slow with birds rising, or when drawing up to a dog pointing, carry the gun with the muzzle slightly raised, the barrels level, the left side of the stock against the right hip-bone.

When standing for driven birds, hold the muzzle well up, the butt resting against the front of the right thigh, and the right barrel slightly inclined downwards.

If you see birds on the wing at a short distance coming directly towards you, hold the gun a little away from the body, the muzzle high, and the arms partly extended, the heel of the stock just level with the inside of the right elbow. You can then put the gun instantly to the shoulder as the game comes within shot.

---

[1] As this is rather a tiring way of carrying a gun, though a very usual one, it will be found a considerable relief to the arm if the shooter has a strip of material to match his dress, 2 inches broad and 6 inches long, down the right side of his coat, just conveniently placed for his right hand. The ends of the strip being sewn to the coat, a loop is formed that acts like a sling to the hand, and greatly eases the weight of the gun.

If rabbit shooting in covert, hold the butt between the arm and the right side, the right hand grasping the handle of the gun, the left well *forward* along the barrels, as it *always should be* when aiming (or even when *about* to aim), the muzzle pointing downwards and straight to the front.[1]

Now a few lines about the actual safety of a gun from accident through an obstruction in the barrels. It is an error to suppose that a barrel will, as a matter of course, burst through *any* foreign substance stopping up its barrels.

What *will* burst a barrel is a stoppage representing a certain amount of weight; for instance, I have known a barrel split from the joint of a cleaning rod being carelessly left in the barrel by a keeper after cleaning the gun, and which was unsuspectingly fired off. I have also split a gun-barrel, for the sake of experiment, by placing a charge of shot, wadded both sides, half way up the barrel. A few inches of snow or *wet* earth in a barrel will also burst a gun, as such substances are compressed by the explosion of the powder instead of being driven out in the form of a bolt.

[1] Do not allow your loader to carry a gun or guns *over his shoulder* if the ground is *rough* or slippery; as, should he trip up, he may very likely smash a stock short off at the handle, and break his head too! Guns are best carried at the 'trail' over uneven ground, then they can be dropped instantly in case of necessity: and without damage, instead of being involuntarily jerked from the shoulder.

I therefore advise the young shooter, before he fires a shot on commencing a day's sport, to look through his barrels without fail, and to make a point of doing so should he have a *missfire*; as sometimes it has happened—once to myself—that with a nitro-compound there had been no missfire, but the cap had in some way failed to explode the charge, yet had developed sufficient force to drive the wads and shot partly up the barrel. Should another cartridge be fired in such a case, an accident is more than probable.

In concluding this letter, I will say that the first and strongest recommendation of a young shooter is his reputation for being an *undeniably safe shot*; and it is well for him to realise that to be an accurate shot is not of nearly so much real importance, when shooting, as being a safe shot. Many shooters, I imagine, will agree with me when I write that the number of shots one sees fired from year to year that *might* have been dangerous, and *ought* to have caused accidents—but which, by sheer good luck and nothing else, did not—are more numerous than pleasant, more exciting than interesting.

LETTER IX

ON KILLING GAME, AND SHOOTING GENERALLY, IN A SPORTSMANLIKE MANNER

FAIR SHOOTING

BECAUSE a shooter is a crack shot, it by no means follows that he is an accomplished sportsman; as there are men, downright bad shots, who are capital fellows and real sportsmen in every sense of the word, whilst there are good shots who are the reverse; for though a shooter may bring his game down with unfailing accuracy, he may yet lack the qualities essential to a true sportsman. Without doubt it is very pleasant to kill with certainty, and it shows great skill to do so, yet I do not envy the shooter, however straight his powder may be, who is a mere 'killing machine,' and who does not rejoice in observing the many elements of instruction and pleasure incidental to a day's shooting.

I consider the *first* idea paramount in the mind of a real sportsman is to avoid *wounding his game* as much as lies in his power, and, when by mischance his game *is* wounded, to do his utmost to *retrieve it quickly*, and thus prevent unnecessary suffering and perhaps a lingering death.

A man who is endowed with a true feeling of sport will always endeavour to give his game a chance—I can think of no better word to express what I mean—as much from the good old English feeling of fair play to all and everything as from any other reason; and in a day's shooting it is curious how often this question of fair play, whether to the game or to one's fellow-shooters, comes to the front, and how easy it is to detect a shooter who is imbued with the right feeling of a sportsman from one who is not. But enough of this moralising. Let me, instead, allude to how a young shooter should behave to the game and to his companions. Two important faults for him to guard against are long shots and shots too near. Nothing looks so bad, or of course spoils game more, whether bird or beast, than killing it but a few yards from the gun; in the first case a cloud of feathers and a rag of bones and flesh, in the second the front and hind quarters held together by the skin of the back, or, perhaps, the head blown half off—an occurrence that makes one long at the time to dig a hole and bury all evidence of such a disgrace.

SHOTS TOO NEAR

Always allow a bird rising in front, especially a large bird like a pheasant, to reach a fair distance, say 25 yards, and, if possible, in the case of a rabbit, 18 yards. I mean, do not fire under these distances, even if, by restraining your trigger, you lose a chance of killing. It is far more sportsmanlike to allow the game to escape, than, by too close shooting, to bag it in a worthless state for food. In the case of *driven* birds, such as grouse or partridges, it is another affair, as *they* can be killed without risk of damage at a closer distance, for, being small birds, they do not receive many pellets, and when coming towards the shooter their plumage is a great protection to them; but recollect that at a range at which a driven partridge or a grouse can be killed without spoiling, a pheasant might be made mince-meat of, even with a cylinder-gun.

In regard to rabbits. they have, I admit, on occasions, to be killed somewhat near, especially if dodging about in fern or brambles. In this case aim straight for the *head*, and do not commit the cruel though not uncommon enormity of firing at the place where you see the leaves stirring, as you are then just as liable to blow off the hindquarters of poor bunny as to hit him in the head. A rabbit is a plucky and sporting little beast, and, if he *has* to be killed, should be treated mercifully with sudden death, yet not fired at so near as to spoil his flesh for the table.

One-third, at least, of the rabbits that are shot in covert are spoilt, and are worth little in consequence. This often results from the system of 'five hundred rabbits ought to be killed to-day, and five hundred must be killed, if possible'; and killed they are, whether at a fair distance or at the very toes of the shooters, and a large amount of good food is wasted from being shot to pieces.

If birds rise too near, it is an ugly habit to put your gun up and follow them with the muzzle till they reach a reasonable distance. Acting thus may, besides, concentrate your attention on the aim to such an extent as to prevent you from noticing the position of your friends, or any other shots that offer. Keep the gun down till the game is at a sporting range; then put it up quickly and fire. If a fellow-shooter bangs off whilst you are allowing a bird to reach a fair distance, and afterwards remarks he imagined you did not see it, or inquires why you did not fire, reply, 'Because I particularly dislike to see game spoilt by close shooting, and I was giving it a little law before bringing it down.'

SHOTS TOO FAR

I now come to long shots; these are more cruel than shots fired too close, and just as wasteful. Occasionally a very long shot is a successful one, and this encourages the shooter to continue in his thoughtlessness; but he little knows, for every bird he kills at long distances, how many he wounds that fly away to die, or to waste into mere skeletons that are no use for food when they are found limping about, or perhaps, instead of being found, are worried by some prowling cat or fox.

Even when very long shots seem successful, it is frequently the case that the game is not gathered; for, though the spectators on such occasions may exclaim, 'What a splendid shot it was!' no shot is a splendid one when the game goes unretrieved, as, oftener than not, is the case after these 'gallery' performances. If the admirers of a long shot troubled to inquire at the time, they would generally find an addition to the bag could not be counted; and though it is, no doubt, a sad spectacle to witness game blown to pieces by being shot too near, yet I would much sooner this occurred than see it escape in a wounded condition; for, at all events, in the former case the shooter is the loser—in the latter it is the game that suffers.[1]

[1] Young shooters are rather prone to describe their supposed long shots, and generally commence to do so with curious similitude of phrase, such as 'You never saw in your life such a shot as I killed the other day!' and, strange to say, all these long shots we hear of are at 70 yards—rarely under or over that distance. It seems as if this was a general length that fitted them all. The fact is, there is not one shooter in a score who can guess with approximate accuracy the correct distance of a long shot. 'That bird was 50 yards, another was 60 yards; one I killed the other day, an extraordinary long one, was 70 yards,' and so on, are statements we not seldom hear. A pheasant, grouse, or partridge, perhaps rises or crosses at 45 yards, is struck by the shot—in fact, killed—at 50 yards, and slopes down wind to 65 yards. As it lies on the ground (though, if it does not run, it may have rebounded or fluttered another 5 yards) it looks an immensely long shot, and the happy shooter who killed it exclaims, 'Keeper, just step the distance from me to that bird.' Off goes

The *grand* object with all winged game is to see it fall dead to the ground, having *died in the air* — the head

Velveteens with solemn face and tread, and shouts out when he reaches the game, '80 yards, sir, every "hinch" of it,' the sly rogue having probably added 10 yards or so, as he has no doubt a private reason for gratifying the shooter's vanity. For the rest of the day and half the night 'Did you see that wonderful shot that I made at a cock pheasant?' is a query often heard. I sometimes *read*, though I have never *seen* such performances, of first-rate marksmen killing *regularly* up to ranges of 50 and 60 yards, or even more. I only hope I may live to see it done. Of course, very long shots can be *sometimes* made at easy birds flying low and from the shooter, as at partridges rising before him; but it is simply nonsense to imagine that, at *all-round game*, shots at such distances can be frequently effected with success by anyone, I do not care who he is. Even at the long, low, straight-away, or, easier still, at the low, slightly crossing birds, the spot where the bird first dropped, as may be seen by the feathers on open ground, is not generally within ten yards of the supposed distance. I do not consider a bird that flutters down, or drops in the form of a runner, but one that falls *dead under the spot at which it was killed*. An old friend of mine (he will smile when he reads this, as he is quite of my way of thinking *now*) used constantly to pace his long shots, and, what is more, made pretty little diagrams of them in a pocket book: and how often he fired these shots again over his smoking-room fire is best known to himself; for, like the true sportsman he is, he never paraded his success or made notes thereon in the field, save when out alone. It occurred to me one day, however, as bad luck would have it, to test his stride; he is not a short man either, being quite the average height. I induced him to pace 65 yards on level ground, in twelve different places, sticks being put to mark each length as completed. The infallible measuring-chain being run over the length, I found the supposed 65 yards in nine cases averaged 58 yards, and in the other three cases 57 yards only. That the above applies to the measurement of most long shots, particularly on uneven ground, I have no doubt. It is curious what *apparently* long, and yet what really *short* paces, a man can step when he wishes to measure a long shot fired by himself; and yet what *very* long steps the same man can stride when he is testing a long shot by someone else. One of the first lessons for a young shooter to learn is, when a long shot is likely to be a successful one, down, and the wings collapsed and clapped together like the lid of a box. Birds that slope down and run, or fall at a distance wounded, are *not* fine shots, however far the game and the shooter were apart when the latter fired. These are merely half-killed birds, that probably require the assistance of dogs and men to bring them to bag—to say nothing of the waste of time incurred in searching for them.

Sometimes, I fear, the good marksmen are most to blame in firing at game at impossible distances. Such men, rarely failing to drop their game at ordinary ranges, look upon a long shot as a subject for experiment, similar to a difficult and uncertain stroke at billiards. Their aim being true they seldom miss; but those three or four feathers that come floating down after the shot is fired tell a sad tale to one who knows. Very long shots, say at 60 to 70 yards, *when* successful, are, after all, nothing but flukes, and are small proof of a gun's power or a man's aim. The pattern of the shot is so wide, at such extravagant distances, that it is not difficult to hit the mark; but if the game is killed on the spot, it is the result of perhaps one pellet having struck the head—a mere accident that may occur once in twenty shots, though the bird be wounded almost every time; for there is

and when it is *not*, and, in the latter case, to restrain his trigger-finger! For instance, a bird that offers a 'tail shot' as it flies away low will rarely be dropped dead at 40 yards, its vital parts being unassailable; though the same bird *crossing* at that distance may fall like a stone, from being struck in the head and neck!

always a likelihood, even at 70 yards, of two or three pellets striking the body of a bird, without sufficient force to kill, yet with enough velocity to manufacture a 'cripple.'

The owner of an estate will usually take care not to wound his own game by firing long shots; and a young shooter should be equally careful not to do it for him. An inferior shot is always liable to wound from incorrect aiming; but this is excusable if he fired at a reasonable range : and in his case it cannot be helped, though he may be assisted by a good marksman placed near him. But firing at game at long ranges likely to wound, whether the sportsman be a good or a bad shot, is unsportsmanlike—more so than shooting at game too near; as in the latter case, though it may be spoilt, it is, at all events, killed on the spot, and saved needless suffering.

THE ETIQUETTE OF THE SHOOTING-FIELD

Fair play towards fellow-shooters is a good quality in a young shooter. If, for instance, a bird rises before him in covert, and offers a low and easy, I may say stupid, shot, he should certainly not fire if another shooter happens to stand forward ; as by the time the game reaches the latter it will probably afford him a high and sporting mark for his gun. Such little compliments as these tend to good-fellowship out shooting, and are usually repaid with interest when the time comes.

Be very careful not to fire at a bird that rises nearer to another shooter than yourself; or which is a fair shot for your friend and a long one for you; or at a bird that rises too far from or too near you, and which, if left alone, will afford your neighbour a fair mark. Above all things, avoid anything approaching jealous shooting, even though your companions may be foolish enough to indulge in it; *jealousy* makes shooting *a very dangerous sport.*[1]

On no account should you fire at game till the man to whom the first chance at it properly belonged has discharged both barrels. Then, if it offers you a fair shot, you can have a try: though, if you kill, you had better half-apologise for doing so, and account for your success through the bird having given you an easy chance; for to 'wipe a man's eye' may be all very pleasant for you, but the man who has had his 'eye wiped' is not, perhaps, so satisfied—especially if he be a much older sportsman or confessedly a superior shot to yourself. So, if you are fortunate in doing this latter feat, do it delicately, I advise.

It is well for a young shooter to recollect, if he is one of a party, that he cannot always be in the best

---

[1] I *hate* a really jealous man in the shooting-field! His motto is, so long as *he* has his fling, and obtains plenty of shots, the game and the other guns may go to the devil—all go right or all go wrong.

place for obtaining shots, and that he will have to take his turn with the other sportsmen and trust to his luck, and certainly not endeavour, if he is in an unfavourable position, to try and better it without directions from the person in authority. In a well-organised shooting day it is the object of the host to deal out the best places to his friends in turn, whatever their rank or powers of marksmanship may be; and should a bad shot chance to enjoy the best place, a good marksman can always be placed behind him to back him up and prevent the game escaping. I recollect hearing on one occasion of a head keeper placing the noble lords continually in the best places in a day's shooting, till at length one of the party, without a handle to his name, losing patience at being always sent to walk up with the beaters, exclaimed, in a well-assumed injured tone, 'Where am I to go this time, keeper? Perhaps you are not aware I'm a banker, and the fifth son of a bishop!'

It is very unsportsmanlike to edge up to another gun who is enjoying plenty of shooting, with the object of sharing his luck and taking some of his shots, unless your assistance is requested, as it may be, if the game rises too fast for your neighbour to kill a good percentage. Nor is it ever a correct proceeding for a shooter to change his place, especially when standing for driven birds, even should he be able to kill more by doing so. It is best for him to previously inquire if he may move in case of the game breaking away out of his reach; else, should a young shooter take it upon himself to alter his position, he may hear hard words spoken to him for having intercepted the birds from being driven in a proper direction for future sport.

When walking in line, a shooter cannot well alter his course, unless he does so wilfully. He should be cautious to keep in line. Few lag behind, but some men *will gallop* forward of the rest. *Nothing* seems to cure them of this annoying habit; whether they do so under the mistaken idea that they procure more shots, or for some other reason, has always been a mystery to me. By walking ahead of a line of guns, though but a few yards forward, a shooter generally drives the birds, as they rise, to either side of him, for the other guns to kill. This is of no consequence, as it serves him right; but he also often prevents his companions from killing the game through his being in the line of fire—shots that neither he nor they can safely take by reason of the irregular line caused through one gun marching ahead of the others.

This sort of behaviour is always looked upon with disapprobation by other sportsmen, as, whether correct in their surmises or not, it gives them the idea that the man who persistently walks forward of the line is endeavouring to jockey his fellow-shooters, and obtain more than his fair share of the sport.

It is not an uncommon habit with a young sportsman, should a bird rise or fly past when two or more shooters are standing together, to be the first to blaze off. Unless the game is palpably his shot, either from its or his position, he should not fire. If it is as much another gun's shot as it is his, he had better leave it alone, and, to prevent the shot being lost through mutual hesitation cry, 'Yours' to his neighbour—just as when fielding at cricket a 'catch' may come to two fielders, either of whom could hold the ball if left to do so without interference.

When out shooting with one friend, be sure you do not fire at the same birds as he does, else your four barrels may bring down but a brace out of a covey rising between you, and these, moreover, so riddled with shot as to be only fit for soup. Take the birds in the covey that are *nearest* to you, whether you be walking or standing. If you are on the right of your friend you will take the right-hand birds, and he the left-hand ones, or the reverse, according to your respective positions. When walking in line, this equally applies to the gun on your right and the one on your left.

It is from a little want of knowledge on the part of shooters as to how the game, as it rises, should be divided among their guns, that it so often occurs, when a couple of fairly easy birds and one or two very easy are flushed at the same time, that the contents of the sportsmen's barrels are showered into the latter, and the former fly away unharmed, when, by a little exercise of judgment, all the birds might have been killed. For the above reason a man may be a good shot, and yet not be so *successful* as another man, of perhaps less accurate aim, who, from his better discrimination of the position of the game, takes full advantage of every chance that offers.

A young sportsman's reputation in connection with shooting can be easily spoilt: one or two dangerous or unsportsmanlike shots, and the argument of the proverbial dog with a bad name holds good. There is no excuse for the former style of shot; though for the latter an apology, and future care not to repeat the mistake may set matters straight.

There are more people in a party of shooters who watch with critical eyes the behaviour of an inexperienced shot than he suspects; and let me tell him he should take just as much care not to fire too near a beater as if the latter were a 'prince of the blood.' One of the neatest hints I ever heard of to be more careful in their aim was given to his friends by a host who printed on his game cards, after the usual list of pheasants, hares, rabbits, &c., *Keepers, beaters, dogs, windows!*

I have seen shooters, who though they never aimed near a friend's person, yet would kill rabbits all round the legs of the beaters, as if the lives of the latter were of secondary consideration.

The most unfortunate and unpleasant thing that can occur to a young shooter, after he has fired a careless shot, is to hear the cry of 'Who fired that shot?' then to see a beater limping out of covert, and be forced to admit *who* fired the shot, and have to hand out a guinea as a solatium for the present, with the chance of a doctor's bill looming in the future—to say nothing of the sportsman's reputation as a safe marksman being irretrievably damaged.

In a day's shooting, the shooters are the actors whose every act is criticised, and the assistants are the audience in the theatre of sport; and very critical and capable observers the latter usually are too.

There are, however, many points of etiquette in the shooting field that require to be learnt intuitively, and from experience rather than from print. For example, never call attention to your own skill; this can easily be seen by your friends without your impressing it upon them; doing so only leads to the conclusion that to shoot well is an unusual and not a frequent attainment on your part. Nor should you make excuses for missing; explanations of the latter kind are absurd if you are a poor marksman, and if you are a good shot they are not required, as everybody fails to kill at times. Some shooters—good shots—apparently look upon missing as a crime, and fancy all present notice their failures; though probably the other guns do not care a straw one way or the other, and are much too intent upon their own performances to criticise those of their neighbours.

The shooters who are the worst marksmen generally make the most excuses, as if it were quite an exceptional occurrence for them to miss at all. I call to mind the story of the gentleman—a notably bad shot—who missed in fine style all day, and who, grumbling furiously at every failure, finally lost his temper completely, and exclaimed to his own keeper, who was attending him, 'I can't shoot a bit to-day,' and was met with the crushing reply, 'You *shoots* well enough, Squire, but you *hits* nowt.'

There are certain rules you should always adhere to when shooting. For instance, if you are walking a covert out towards other guns posted forward outside, never fire at low birds that rise in front of you, however tempting the shots appear; nor should you even fire at rabbits, unless they are near and the forward guns are at a safe distance. In the same way, if a forward gun yourself, on no account fire at low birds coming towards you out of a covert, and only at ground game between you and the guns walking up when the latter are at a perfectly safe distance; in any case, it is better to stand quite still, and take your shots as the game passes overhead or behind you.

Counting the game you have killed at a stand, or in a day's sport, and letting others know of your success, is always unsportsmanlike, unless it is a matter of general conversation or inquiry. Killing more game than anybody else is oftener the result of good luck than of good shooting. A young shooter seldom counts correctly, and the more he adds up as his total (he does not often subtract), the less he leaves for the other guns. I give an amusing example of this that I can vouch for. One of the best shots in England invited several young shooters to his grouse moor; the bag was a heavy one, and all save the host were full of their own shooting, and what each gun had killed as his share. After a deal of dispute as to how this shooter had brought to bag fifty birds, and that one sixty, they finally arranged everything to their satisfaction—a satisfaction somewhat marred when the host, who had to every eye shot splendidly, quietly remarked that 'he was afraid he should have to give up shooting, because, during the day, he had fired at least a hundred shots, and after subtracting the bag accounted for by his friends from the real total brought in by the keepers, it appeared that he had *only killed three birds.*'

A young shooter needs cure himself of any tendency to excitement in the field, such as may occur to him when the game is in abundance. It is always the man who is cool and collected who is not only the safest shot, but the one who kills his game in the most sportsmanlike style. However plentiful the game may be, an absence of excitement will certainly enable a shooter to use his judgment in discriminating between safe and dangerous shots, and what he ought to fire at and what he had best leave alone. Such a man will also make up his mind instantly, whilst the nervous sportsman will point his gun and take it down, and point it again, and then perhaps hesitate between one bird and another, and finally pounce upon somebody else's shot, or else fire at a bird too near or too far, though a fair shot offered in front of his nose.

It is thoroughly sportsmanlike behaviour of a shooter who, being the host, takes a 'back seat,' and places himself where he may rather have the worst of the sport than the best. When he shoots with his friends, he will probably have every chance of a 'front seat.' I like to see a host manage his shooting, rather than participate in it, and throughout the day arrange that his friends have the best of the sport. To my mind, there is on these occasions just as much, if not, indeed, more, pleasure in acting the part of head keeper and seeing that all goes well, than there is in slaying your own game.[1]

Foolish and boasting wagers are most reprehensible and unsportsmanlike, and are not seldom indulged in by young shooters. Such talk as 'I'll back myself to

---

[1] As far as the question of real sporting interest is concerned, and putting on one side their respective values, I would sooner possess an estate of fair size than own half a county. In the former case a landlord can supervise the rearing and preservation of his game; he will be able to learn its habits and favourite localities, and hence realise the amount of sport he is likely to show his friends. In the latter case, a great deal has by necessity to be taken for granted, or is a matter of surmise, as on very extensive properties the keepers alone *really* know what the woods and fields contain in the way of game, especially in regard to distant beats.

hit this or that mark,' 'Your gun does not shoot so hard as mine,' and so forth, usually leads to ill-feeling, if not risk.

I recollect hearing of two young sportsmen who had a violent dispute as to the capabilities of their guns, when finally one said, 'I dare stand behind the corner of the house and hold out my hand, and I will bet you a sovereign your gun will not put a pellet into it at 50 yards, and here is one of my cartridges to try with.'

Now this very clever youth had carefully drawn the shot and substituted sand, and laughed in his sleeve as his companion carefully paced the distance. But his friend, being of a compassionate turn towards what he considered the folly of his fellow-shooter, and not wishing to hurt him, as he thought, more than necessary—for he felt confident in his aim and the power of his gun—substituted a No. 10 snipe cartridge he chanced to have in his pocket instead of the one supposed to contain No. 5 shot which his friend had given him. The result may be imagined, though the punishment was, I consider, deserved.

LETTER X

ON CORRECT AIMING—PRACTICAL

THE practice and theory of aiming correctly permits of endless argument; and next to aiming safely and shooting generally in a sportsmanlike manner, the gift of accuracy with his gun is of most importance to a shooter's career; for to kill his game with regularity and neatness is probably the chief object of his ambition—the two former attributes being more necessities than attainments.

It is all very well to talk of fine, old-fashioned sport with setters and pointers, and of seeking your game by their aid in what is often alluded to as if it were the only sportsmanlike manner. That is well enough; but, on the other hand, we desire to kill the game when found, and would do so every time we fire were we able to; and I expect that to nine out of ten shooters the fact of bringing their game down dead is the greatest pleasure they experience when afield, and their failure to accomplish this their greatest disappointment.

It is a very satisfactory thing to find, for instance, a woodcock, or a wild pheasant, or a covey of partridges, after half an hour's hard work and careful search; but all the pleasure vanishes in a moment if the shooter bangs off both barrels without success; and he then, likely enough, looks upon his previous cleverness in hunting down his birds as so much time wasted, though up to the moment of firing he held quite another opinion.

There are people who will almost declare that the pleasure of seeing their dogs work, and the mere finding of the game, is about all they really care for, and that skill with the gun is quite a secondary consideration, a mere mechanical act, and an accessory that cannot be dispensed with. I confess I am not one of these one-sided enthusiasts. I like to see game well brought to the gun, or the gun well taken to the game, with equal pleasure; but I *do* like to see the game well killed, when the chance of killing does occur.

Skill with the gun is in itself a delightful and absorbing accomplishment; and it is foolish to say it is not, as it would be similar nonsense to insist that there is no enjoyment to be derived from the expert handling of a cricket bat, a billiard cue, a racket, a bow, or any other implement requiring dexterous use, which depends for its success upon the excellence of the individual performer who wields it, and which is often devoid of outside elements of sport.

Some men shoot well from their first lesson with

a gun; but such are born marksmen, and have not so much acquired their skill by practice as by natural gift. These few fortunates fire off their guns as if they took no care in aiming, and yet drop their game dead in fine style. On the other hand, there are men who take the *utmost care*, and who are *models* of perseverance, and hit next to nothing. To the former, any alteration of style would probably ruin their capabilities of shooting correctly; in fact, they want no teaching, and I do not write for such experts as these, who, whether they handle a gun, a rod, a bat, or a cue, appear to take to it kindly and adroitly from boyhood. It is a different matter, however, in regard to the man or boy who, as an inferior shot, is learning to shoot, or who, after years of practice, does not improve or know how to do so; it is such as these that I hope to assist.

How does a good shot aim? He cannot tell you himself, because so many personal attributes are necessary to his success; his hand, his eye, his figure, and his brain all have their separate duties to perform; and they are all performed momentarily, without *apparent* consideration, though done instinctively and together, and well-nigh methodically.

Your good shot picks up a gun and says: 'Now, watch me; I always stand like this. I put up my gun, take no particular sight, and, bang! down comes the bird.' You do the same on the first opportunity, or *think* you do; but, alas! you nevertheless may not notice much improvement in your shooting; and perhaps down the bird does *not* come as often as you imagine it *should* do, considering the careful plans you have matured for its execution.

It is never amiss, however, to copy a good model; and if you have the chance, observe the motions of a first-rate shot, in the field, not in the gunroom, and notice his style. It will very rarely be a bad style, and imitation of it *may* assist you considerably. But to do this successfully you need to be in figure and height somewhat similar to your model; though, as a short, stout man, for example, could never acquire the easy and probably graceful attitudes of a tall, slight one, the former will be obliged to do the best he can for himself under different conditions.

Now, putting on one side, for the present, powers of sight, readiness of hand and brain, and other questions, I may say that there are, at overhead and crossing shots (the *only really* difficult ones), three distinct methods of aiming, the causes and effects of which I will endeavour to describe.

FIRST SYSTEM (*a difficult one*)

To aim ahead of the game in the first instance without previously sighting it with the gun, and send the charge of shot so as to intercept the mark as the latter reaches the imaginary point in the atmosphere which the shooter has decided to be the one where the game and the shot from his gun should meet—the gun being stationary at the moment of firing.

SECOND SYSTEM (*a good one*)

To aim straight and fair at the game on first putting the gun to the shoulder; then to jerk the muzzle the supposed necessary distance ahead, according to pace and flight, and also pull trigger with a stationary gun.

THIRD SYSTEM (*the best*)

To aim just forward of the *head* of the game at a *short* range, and *its own length* ahead at a fairly *long* one, and swing (in the case of shots at ordinary ranges, jerk) the muzzle in line with the flight of the object; then fire, without stopping (there's the rub) the quick, lateral movement of the gun, and without dwelling a moment on the aim.[1]

Except when game is fired at flying low towards the shooter or going straight from him—when killing is an easy affair, and almost like a sitting shot— these three methods comprise the principles of aiming. I will take them *seriatim*

---

[1] The three words *swing, jerk,* and *direct* (as applied to a gun when aiming), that occur in this letter, require some explanation so as not to seem contradictory. The word *jerk* and the word *swing*

COMMENTS ON FIRST SYSTEM OF AIMING

In the first example, the great difficulty is the act of firing into space away from the game—an unknown space, too; for it takes a rare good marksman to judge in half a thought how many feet forward he should fire at a bird flying across the sky—when he has to keep his eyes on the mark, in order to see which way its flight inclines, and has also to decide accurately on the imaginary point in the air which he desires his shot to reach at the exact moment his bird does so too. This is a difficult feat to accomplish with certainty in the case of a bird, though with ground game a fairly easy one, as there is *then*, from the nature of the surroundings, perhaps somewhat of a guide to go by in the matter of firing ahead.

This system is all very well in theory, but I believe in practice it is seldom accomplished with regularity; and though shooters may fancy they achieve success

are practically similar in the sense in which I use them. For instance, the gun-muzzle will have to be *jerked* to enable it to keep just forward of the flight of a bird crossing rapidly at an *ordinary* distance: to speak of swinging the gun in such case would imply too slow and long a lateral movement of the barrels by the shooter. At a long shot, however, the gun-muzzle *can* be momentarily *swung* with the line of flight, as the longer the distance the more time the shooter usually has to aim, and the slower the game appears to fly; hence the word *swing* is *then* the more applicable expression to use. In regard to the word *direct*, I use it to imply that the shooter should rather direct the barrels of his gun toward the game he wishes to kill, than that he should take a rifle-like aim with the actual sight of his gun.

by endeavouring to allow an exact distance forward of their game, I expect that at the moment of pulling trigger they rarely put their intentions into effect. What is more, I am convinced that, by attempting to fire into empty space just the supposed necessary number of feet that the game will have traversed by the time the shot should strike it, a shooter is very likely to be led into acquiring a habit of pitching his gun forward the same distance for nearly all the crossing shots he fires, whether near or distant; as it would take a clever fellow to arrange during the twentieth part of a second whether he should put up his gun-muzzle so as to send the shot 4 feet, 3 feet, or 18 inches ahead of a crossing bird.

It is all very fine to say a correct judgment of atmospheric space can be formed instinctively. Though it may be done by long practice in the case of first-rate shots, or by a fortunate chance in the case of bad or average marksmen, still, the attempt to rule out feet and inches in thin air is very liable to bother a *young* shooter exceedingly, and to cause every shot he fires to become an *experiment*, in the *success* of which he does not feel confident.

Few can instantaneously decide the correct amount to aim forward when this amount varies with every shot, according as the game is parallel, slanting, crossing, or overhead—not to speak of such items as pace of flight, strength of wind, distance, and other considerations, all of which are most difficult to judge correctly on the instant, as there is so little time for considering them. The fact is, a shooter must *act*, not *think*, when aiming; and the less he is obliged to consider his shots the better will he shoot. It is frequently the bird you see approaching in the far distance, and that grants you as much leisure for deliberation as a move at chess or a stroke at billiards, and which you carefully prepare to slay with all the certainty imaginable, that, when it *does* come within range, seems to dash overhead without giving you any time to carry out your well-laid plans for killing it as dead as a door-nail!

How often do we hear the remark, after a clean miss : ' If I had but fired 4 feet in front of that bird I should have killed, but I only gave him about 3 feet.' What the difference between 3 feet and 4 feet looks like in front of a bird flying rapidly through the air at 30 to 40 yards distance, I do not credit anyone knowing. Nor do I believe the *accurate* calculation of a forward space in the air is ever attempted by successful marksmen ; or that the power of doing so is a lesson that can be learnt by mortal eyes with sufficient correctness to be of *real* service to a young shooter when aiming.

The shooter who vows he aims in front of his mark, and declares that he pulls the *trigger* when there is a clear space of what he has pre-arranged it is necessary to allow between his gun-muzzle and the game, does not, I believe, *really* carry out his theory once in a score times; but, from his habit of aiming well forward, he is more likely to drop his bird though he pull the trigger as its head is just crossing towards the muzzle of the gun. That the shooter often fires his gun *actually* at the point *ahead* of the game he *fancies* he does, I do not credit. In this we see, however, the difference between a bad and a good shot. The former, even should he aim well forward, may fail to fire till the mark has crossed the open space he has allowed it; the latter, besides hitting off the correct line of the bird's flight, will fire so much quicker that he actually *does* shoot more or less forward, or into the head of the game (though *not* to the exact extent he imagines), instead of shooting behind, by hesitating over his aim and hanging on the trigger.

COMMENTS ON SECOND SYSTEM OF AIMING

That the first system of aiming is a quicker method than the second, *when* a shooter can practise it, there is no doubt; as in the latter case he is forced to take two sights at his game—one when he first covers it with the muzzle, and a second when he fires at the spot in the air he *hopes* the object and his charge of shot will reach simultaneously. At the same time, the second system is a *far* more *reliable* one than the first, and also easier to carry out, *especially* in the event of driven birds passing *overhead*, as, having once aligned the mark, and realised its correct line of flight, the shooter is more likely to hit it than if he had taken no first sight at his bird.

COMMENTS ON THIRD SYSTEM OF AIMING

We now come to the third and best system, which is, at ordinary sporting ranges, say up to 30 yards, to aim just forward of the head of the game, and jerk the gun with its line of flight, and pull the trigger *without* checking the very short lateral movement of the gun—a plan that has one *great* advantage, for no calculation is required of the shooter in the matter of empty space, his gun muzzle being, as regards aiming, close to the mark from first to last. This system of aiming is thoroughly sound, *if* carried out; it is this carrying of it out that is the difficulty: but then it is a difficulty that can, or at all events *may*, be overcome by manipulation and *not* by calculation, and is in conséquence a system I strongly advise the adoption of, and one which, by practice, will eventually be the most likely to assist a young shooter in becoming a good shot.

The hard part of the performance is to jerk the gun in line with the game, to fire *quickly*, without any noticeable dwelling on the aim, and to fire without in the least *checking* the lateral jerk of the gun *as the trigger is pulled.*

You can easily test your power of doing this for yourself. Direct two men to stand 30 yards apart, and bowl a cricket-ball along the ground, so that it passes, in line with its course, two upright sticks five yards apart. You will probably find you can easily follow the course of the ball from stick to stick with your gun to the shoulder. Now aim in a similar way, and, keeping the same swing on the gun as before, pull a trigger when the ball is half-way between the sticks. What happens? This. On snapping the lock the muzzle of your gun will drop behind the ball; and if the ball had been a bird you would have 'shot well behind,' and not even feathered the tail of a cock pheasant.

To acquire a correct habit of aiming with a 'lateral jerk,' you should be able to see your gun-muzzle just forward of the ball during its flight, *after* pulling the trigger. If *this* occurs, it will prove you kept up the necessary movement at the moment of firing; *then*, if the ball were the head of a bird at reasonable range, you would have scored a kill. By frequent practice of this kind, as well as at every bird you see on the wing, small or large, you will eventually conquer the great difficulty in all aiming at crossing game—the perverse tendency to check the lateral movement of the gun on pulling trigger.

When you can keep up this 'swing,' or, rather, 'jerk,' throughout the flight of a ball (or of a bird) moving fast or slow between two points a few yards apart, and are able to pull *both* triggers *quickly*, and yet not drop the gun-muzzle behind the mark on the pull of either, you will find your shooting not a little improved—provided, of course, there was room for improvement.¹

Do not allow the ball, when you are experimenting, to be pitched in the air, as it then appears almost stationary when at the summit of its flight. It is at this turning-point that feats of aiming are performed at pennies, stones, and such articles with a rifle; they are not nearly so difficult as they look, and are of no service when practised with a view to attaining accuracy at game with a gun.

[1] The reason for snapping trigger at the ball as it passes between two upright sticks placed in the ground in line with its course, and a few yards apart, is in order to practise the shooter in firing without any hesitation or dwelling on his aim. He should be able to sight the ball with his gun as it appears past the first stick (the one nearest the thrower), snap the lock, and see the muzzle for just an instant ahead of the mark before the second stick is reached by the latter. If a shooter merely aimed at the ball during any part of its course between the two throwers, he would have no practice in aiming and firing smartly, as is, of course, necessary at game, and he would be sure to acquire the very bad habit of dwelling on his aim.

One of the most difficult shots to succeed in, and one I have never seen regularly accomplished, is at a pheasant that flies high towards a shooter (as he stands in the open) and then wheels at a good speed (with a strong wind) back to the cover from which it was driven, just as it comes into shot. Of course the pheasant that acts thus is describing part of the outline of a circle in its flight, so that if the gun is placed forward of the mark, however slightly, the latter is sure to escape by reason of its twisting continually to one side of the aim.

If the bird is 'dropping' as well as 'curving' it is a still more uncertain shot. The only aim that is likely to be successful at a nasty curving bird, such as I describe, is one that is directed towards the point of the wing that is farthest from the shooter: namely, the one that is *inside* the curve described by the pheasant in its course.

LETTER XI

ON CORRECT AIMING—PRACTICAL (continued)

NOT a little of the success that pertains to jerking a gun in line with crossing game is caused by a correct grasp. Many shooters hold the left hand too near the breech of the gun and the elbow in a cramped and stiff position as a result. The left hand, when the shooter is about to aim, should be stretched along the barrel, the arm nearly straight, and, with a shooter of average stature, the little finger just clear of the fore-end of the stock. It is a bad habit to hold the fore-end in the left hand, and, as the aim is taken, slide the grasp forward, as this causes two motions, when one would do, and be much quicker. The gun should be brought *up* to the aim, with the left arm well extended, and the left hand clear of the fore-end; and the aim should be taken in this position.

Another thing worthy of notice about aiming at crossing shots is, that it is not nearly so easy to direct a gun and fire it when using both hands for this purpose as when *one* hand is used for the former act, and one for the latter. The duty of the right hand is to fire the gun—in fact, pull the trigger; of the left hand, to point the muzzle. If *both* hands are occupied in aiming the gun, as soon as the trigger has to be pulled the right hand contracts and pauses, and causes the left to check the barrels in their forward motion in line with the game. The left hand can easily be trained to do all the work of directing the gun, whilst the right hand performs its duty of firing the charge; and any shooter can easily prove this fact for himself by snapping the locks of an empty gun when moving it laterally.[1]

At the risk of repetition, I will finally state that, if a shooter is puzzled as to how or where to aim at crossing or overhead shots at *ordinary* distances, he should simply and invariably direct his gun just forward of the 'head' or 'beak'—according as ground or winged game be the mark—and endeavour on all occasions to jerk his gun in line with his game, and pull trigger without checking the muzzle at the moment of firing—looking fixedly at his object, with *both* eyes wide open and *head erect*—and he will thus kill more game than by any other method.

---

[1] Just the same argument applies when we throw a fly with a salmon-rod or a double-handed trout-rod. With both hands held close together we have little power to direct the top of the rod so that it places the fly where we wish. With one hand stretched up the butt of the rod we can cast as we please.

XI.   ON CORRECT AIMING (PRACTICAL)

At *fairly long* crossing or high overhead shots a shooter will be equally successful if he aim forward 'the *length* of the bird or beast he wishes to kill, not omitting to jerk his gun as before described. Judging *this* length is quite easy,[1] and a very different affair from calculating feet and inches.

At *long shots* (should he fire such) the shooter can easily train his eye to direct his aim forward *the length of a gun,* swinging his barrels for an instant with the game as a matter of course.[2]

I consider the above is the easiest system of aiming to inculcate in the mind of a young shooter or an

---

[1] The length of a cock pheasant is about 3 ft., which is an ample allowance forward for him as a crossing bird up to 30 yards, always provided the trigger is pulled without checking the jerk of the gun-muzzle in line with his flight.

[2] A shooter should be able to form a very good idea of what a gun-length is in front of a bird, though if he endeavoured to rule out 4 ft. in the air in his mind's eye he might fail to do so. The length of a gun is something material for the imagination to seize upon, as this length is one we are familiar with. Of course, to aim a fixed length forward of long crossing birds that vary in their pace and distance would never do if the gun is *stationary* when the trigger is pulled; on the other hand, if the shooter aims and retains a fixed length ahead of such shots, and this length is about 4 ft., he will kill oftener than miss *if* he *swings* his gun *instead* of keeping it stationary, and fires without checking its lateral movement. It is worth remark, too, that we do not fire a *bullet* at our game, but in the case of a cylinder or medium-choked gun a large circle, that allows for some inaccuracy of aim. See Fig. 6, p. 157.

inferior shot, as it is a practical one, and free from confusing theories of speed and other allowances. In whatever direction the game crosses, whether in the form of rabbits in covert, grouse over dogs, high rocketing pheasants, or driven partridges (the latter the most difficult shooting of all), this advice is equally applicable; and the marksman will at all events feel, if he misses, that his want of success was caused, not by bad judgment of the pace and flight of his game—theories he may never learn the rudiments of—but rather from errors arising from want of practice and confidence in the handling of his gun—faults that are capable of correction.

Shooting behind or pulling the trigger when an overhead or crossing bird has passed the sight taken by the shooter (though his aim be true enough in the first instance) is one of the most difficult faults to cure, but is one that is well worth taking great pains to rectify. Perseverance in this respect is well repaid—a good deal on account of the satisfaction of making clean kills, and a good deal more in order that a shooter may not see that most unsportsmanlike and unpleasant of sights, birds going away with legs hanging down, or falling winged, and ground game creeping forward or to shelter with hind-quarters dragging after them.

How often are we conscious of firing too far in front? Precious seldom, I take it.

Aiming too much ahead is, of course, possible, but

not probable; it is, however, a good fault, as by doing so the shot *may* strike the game. But shooting at the *body*, and *not* the head of game, nearly always means that the shot is too late in reaching the mark, and only wounds with the weak and straggling pellets that fringe the shot-circle.

The very act of always striving to direct the muzzle of the gun just clear of the head of every bird or beast will, in the case of crossing shots, of itself be the means of giving a forward inclination to the aim.

In reference to jerking a gun in line with the mark, I do not in the least intend to convey that the shooter is to *dwell* on his aim, and practise the intolerable and dangerous habit of following the game with his gun to the shoulder; for, in the case of a low shot, it would then be possible for him to cover with the sight the dogs and men in his vicinity. That is quite a different thing from moving his gun with a quick, dashing jerk in line with his mark, and pulling trigger as soon as he realises the muzzle of his gun is forward of the head of the game he desires to kill.

In the case of firing a gun with a lateral jerk on crossing game, if the shooter can do this in the manner I have described, there is no necessity for him, at ordinary distances, to aim several feet in front of the fastest birds that fly past or over him, as the result of giving this swing to the gun is the same in effect as aiming forward.

EASY SHOTS

It is well for a shooter to know that, though a bird may, to all appearance, be flying directly from him, *if* its *head* can be seen it is *really* flying towards the side on which the head appears. A straight shot at the bird might not then bring it to bag. In this case the head should alone be aimed at, so that the shot may meet the real line of flight, as, though the bird may appear to be going straight away, you may depend upon it it is going to the right or left in a curve.

Birds that rise before the shooter and fly straight away are, however, really the simple ones, and are easier at a fair range, owing to the wider spread of the shot, than they are at a short distance—especially with the bullet-like charge thrown by a full-choked gun; such shots require no calculation as to aiming ahead, and little dexterity in pulling trigger so as to kill. Before the era of driven game, easy straightforward shots were the rule; and I can quite understand that the best marksmen of fifty years since killed these with just as much certainty as our best men do now.

Though, at a fairly long range, a wounded bird may result from a straight-away shot, by reason of its being struck behind, still, a clean miss should rarely occur; and till a young shooter can make certain of killing birds flying away from him, at fair range, seven out of every ten times he pulls a trigger, he will not have much success in bringing down driven birds or birds crossing him; for these straight-away shots usually consist, to attain success, in merely placing the sight fair on the object, without any other conditions of aiming; and, for this reason, there are no shots *more useful in testing the fit of a gun.*

It looks well, no doubt, to see a man stop thirty or forty rabbits with scarcely a miss in a level field, or drop dead a score birds in succession that rise in front of his toes—as is the case with grouse or partridges when they sit well at the beginning of the season. But this is no *real* proof of a good marksman: a moderate shot might do *almost* as well; for the man who can kill easy, straightforward birds time after time, may be, nevertheless, a poor performer at all-round game, and frequently miss what to experts would be easy chances.[1]

[1] The shooter who neatly kills a score of easy, straightforward shots in succession is apt to say, 'What a good shot am I,' and to flatter himself that really no one *could* be a much better one! Let our gentleman be placed, however, near a first-class marksman, in a position where all varieties of shots offer, and he will soon have to eat 'humble-pie.' The misses that will occur, and the number of double shots he will have to fire, when firing at rabbits dodging about in turnips or high fern, for instance, will surprise him! Woodcocks darting between trees, wood-pigeons now and then dashing overhead, some driven partridges that almost knock his hat off before he sees them, a few *really* tall pheasants passing to one side of him down wind across a small open space in a thick wood, or maybe some driven grouse flying *high* in a *strong* breeze down hill, and what becomes of the high average of dead birds to single shots that our friend can maintain, when firing at partridges in September in good cover? In all-round shooting, fifteen kills to twenty shots is rarely done. Of

Many of the shots that pigeons offer when flying from traps are straight-away shots of the simplest description; though if the shooter is placed well back, and has to fire very quickly at a fast-springing bird that, on rising, at once inclines its flight to right or left, it is another matter. But it by no means follows that a crack pigeon-shot is successful at game, as in regard to the latter there are many angles of flight which he is unaccustomed to. I have known several examples of this. On the other hand, a good game-shot, with a little practice, is sure to succeed at pigeons from traps, as there is no angle in the flight of the bird which he has not had experience of.

ON THE ATTITUDE OF A SHOOTER

I have before alluded to the fit of a gun, and will now take it for granted that a shooter's gun fits him; for, unless it does, no amount of practice will make him a first-rate shot. I have known men who could shoot *fairly* well with a gun of any shape, but I never knew a really good shot who could shoot his *best* unless his gun fitted him perfectly; as the latter is

course, *if* a shooter obtains a series of chances at even fairly high birds that offer shot after shot at a similar angle and pace, he becomes what may be termed 'set,' just as a batsman masters the pitch of a bowler who does not vary his delivery of the ball; yet a sudden change in the flight of the game, and a full pitched ball, or one that 'shoots,' and the 'gunner' and the cricketer may respectively fail to 'score'!

so completely in touch with his gun that it seems to him almost to come up accurately on the aim of its own accord when he uses it. I merely allude to this subject again in order to impress upon the young shooter how careful he should be to obtain a gun that fits him; this he will soon discover for himself by taking notice if the muzzle comes up easily on his game, whatever the position of the latter may chance to be, whether he takes a steady aim in broad daylight, or whether he has to fling his gun to the shoulder at a passing duck in the dusk without seeing the muzzle at all.

It is also necessary I should point out that an easy, natural position is essential to good aiming, and a shooter should practise to attain it; as the man whose limbs are loose and free will be much more ready with his gun than will the man who stands like a statue when aiming; for stiffness of the figure is most detrimental to quick and correct shooting.

For instance, a shooter who plants both legs firmly on the ground, and, when he fires, grasps his gun as if it were an iron bar, can never change his attitude so rapidly as to direct his aim here and there, as required by the position of the game, with anything like the success of the man whose limbs and muscles are pliable.

Of course, a shooter should be firm on his legs; but this firmness may be the strength of a light and safe balance, rather than the solidity of a young oak;

the left leg always forward, whether for a shot in front, a high-driven shot, or a shot to the right or left.

If you notice a good marksman, you will observe that, in the act of firing, his weight is thrown on the left leg, and that the foot of the other leg acts as a pivot, and but lightly touches the ground. He is not in the least unsteady therefrom, but in reality perfectly balanced, and more or less as it were on springs that enable him to turn his figure to fire quickly in any direction.

The shooter who acquires a stiff attitude will be sure to feel the recoil of his gun more than will the man who is easy and natural in his movements. This is especially noticeable when firing at overhead birds —rocketing pheasants, for instance. In such cases, practise the habit of standing as loosely as possible consistent with a safe balance, so as to offer a yielding spring, to absorb the recoil of your gun. I have known a shooter's collar-bone to be smashed from the mere fact of his stepping on to a stone, off soft ground, to save wet boots, whilst shooting at ducks flying high over; and this, too, with a 12-bore gun. If my friend had remained on the soft, yielding ground, his bones would not have suffered; and the principle applies equally to a rigid attitude when shooting at *all* birds overhead.

ON CORRECT AIMING (PRACTICAL)

THE TRIGGERS, AND A BRUISED FINGER

The pull of the triggers of a gun is a question of great importance in connection with correct aiming. If these offer too much resistance to the finger of a shooter, they will certainly have the effect of causing him to fire 'too late,' and thus to 'shoot behind'; for the extra pressure they require, beyond what is adapted to his touch, results, during his delay in firing, in the game travelling a closer distance than he bargained for towards the point he intended his shot to reach. On the other hand, if his triggers pull too easily, they may cause him to fire before he has completed his aim—the result being then as unsuccessful as dangerous.

Alteration of the pull of the triggers of a gun is an easy matter, and a shooter will soon feel for himself if his gun fires 'too soon' or 'too late,' and return it to his gunmaker for readjustment. The usual pull-off for the triggers is, right 4 lb., left $4\frac{3}{4}$ lb.; and the way to test them is with an ordinary spring balance, such, for instance, as is used by a trout-angler for weighing his fish. The left trigger should always pull off heavier than the right, as the finger has more leverage against the second trigger; and the extra $\frac{3}{4}$ lb. given to the latter equalises the pull of both triggers to the touch of the shooter.

The triggers of a gun, whatever their resistance, should pull off short and sharp, without any draw.

In an inferior gun it sometimes happens that a trigger can be pressed back when the shooter aims without firing, and will remain in this very dangerous condition. Then, when a shot *is* fired, bang goes the gun as if it had a 'hair-trigger.'

Whilst alluding to the triggers of a gun, it is worthy of remark that that greatest of all nuisances, 'a sore finger,' is, nine cases out of ten, the result of a bad-fitting gun. A gun too long in the stock, or too short, will equally cause this unpleasantness. If the bruise is on the second joint of the second finger—a very usual place—it may be caused by the trigger-guard not being sloped sufficiently to slide through the right hand on the recoil taking place, its steep outline striking against the finger instead of sliding over it. A downright bad-fitting gun will, from its being able to jump in the shooter's grasp, be always liable to knock his fingers about.

A gun with a round instead of an oval handle to the stock, as may be seen in second-class workmanship, will also cause bruised fingers, as such a gun is liable to turn in the hands, and then, from not being in a level position, 'bounce' when put to the shoulder and fired.

I have known a friend have his first finger badly bruised from contact with the front trigger on his firing the second. Nothing seemed to remedy this till I had his front trigger put on a hinge, so as to fall forward on being touched. This is a good method in such a case, when all other means fail, and can be easily arranged without in the least affecting the usefulness of the gun or the convenience of the shooter.

A pistol-handle is a *certain* cure for a sore *second* finger, as, from the firm grasp it gives, the hand of the shooter recoils with the gun; though, as I have described in a former letter, a stock thus shaped is detrimental to quick shooting.

I have now treated of the practical part of aiming I have found it a subject most difficult to elucidate as clearly as I would wish. At all events, I have done my best, such as it is, to prevent a young shooter from being known as a three-barrel man—or bang, bang, d——n!

LETTER XII

CORRECT AIMING (continued)—THEORETICAL. (INTENDED TO BE MORE CURIOUS THAN INSTRUCTIVE)

HAVING described in the two previous letters the best method in my experience for the young shooter to adopt to become a successful shot, I will write a little for the particular benefit of those shooters who cannot acquire a habit of jerking the gun just forward of the game in its line of flight, and firing without checking the lateral movement of the muzzle.

This last class of shooter, however difficult or uncertain such a proceeding may be, *must* aim ahead in the case of crossing shots, or he would, of course, fire several feet behind his mark did he aim straight at the latter without any swing on his gun.

The speed of all flying game is very similar, though some birds appear to fly slower than others because they are large, like pheasants, and others seem to fly faster because they are small, like grouse or partridges. Nothing is more deceptive than the

XII. ON CORRECT AIMING (THEORETICAL)   153

pace a bird flies at. I will give an instance. I have often, when wildfowl shooting, seen swans flying, to all appearance, slowly and heavily across the horizon, and in company with them a few ducks, going along as hard as they could, and yet dropping gradually behind—and we all know a wild duck can travel at a good speed; yet a swan never appears to fly at the speed of a wild duck, on account of its great size. I have made many experiments connected with this subject by taking, with a stop-watch, the time occupied by different birds in crossing a field the width of which I knew exactly beforehand, standing myself at one hedge, and a man signalling, by raising a flag at the opposite one, the moment the bird I was timing passed him, and between two posts in line with his eye.

But to revert to my subject. I find a cock pheasant that has been fired at—not to kill, but to alarm—will fly time after time, on a calm day, at the rate of 55 ft. to 65 ft. per second. I will take 60 ft. as his average pace, as this represents just 40 miles an hour, and simplifies my illustration. Now, a charge of $1\frac{1}{8}$ oz. of No. 6 shot, driven by 3 dr. of powder, travels, up to 40 yards, at the mean velocity of about 840 ft. a second; so that, without going into fractions, it may be said that the cock pheasant in question will have flown 8 ft. 6 in. while the shot is travelling from the gun to the bird, provided the latter is crossing the shooter at right angles at 40 yards.

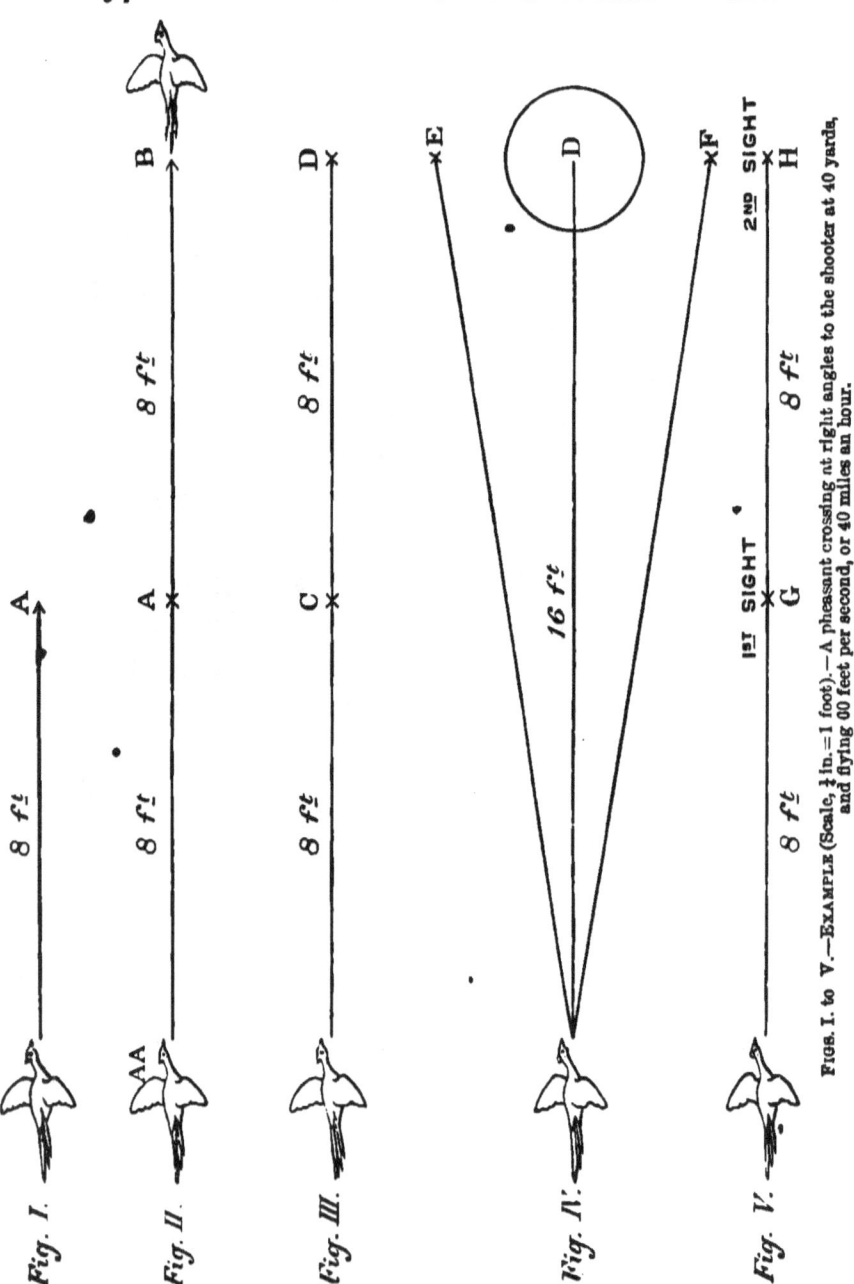

FIGS. I. to V.—EXAMPLE (Scale, ¾ in. = 1 foot).—A pheasant crossing at right angles to the shooter at 40 yards, and flying 60 feet per second, or 40 miles an hour.

This 8 ft. (we will drop the 6 in.) ahead of a fast crossing bird at from 30 yards to 40 yards is a pretty reliable rule—provided the shooter does not hesitate in the *slightest* degree over his *aim*. A bird flying somewhat on a slant with the shooter will not, according to its deviation from the right angle, require so much as an 8 ft. allowance; but, on the other hand, the slanting bird runs more risk of being hit, as it does not travel straight through the circle of shot; for the latter partly follows it up, as the shot-charge from a gun travels in the form of an oval.

FIG. I.—A is the point at which aim was taken by the shooter, so as to allow 8 ft. for the pace of the bird, or the distance it would fly during the actual transit of the shot from the gun.

FIG. II.—A, the point at which aim was taken (as in Fig. I.); but from the shooter dwelling on his trigger one-eighth of a second, by the time the shot left the gun the pheasant would arrive at A; and before the charge could reach the line of flight of the bird the latter would have flown another 8 ft. forward to B, and the shot would arrive at A, just 8 ft. behind the bird, which will have flown 16 ft. from its original position at A A along the line to B. This shows us how easy it is to fire 'too late.'

FIG. III.—It may be asked, 'Why not fire at D, or 16 ft. forward, in the first instance, and allow the 8 ft. from the pheasant to C for hesitation in pulling trigger, and from C to D (also 8 ft.) for the distance the bird would travel during the time expended by the shot in transit, so that bird and charge might meet at D?'

FIG. IV.—The answer to this suggestion is, that the point D (or 16 ft. ahead of the mark) is too far forward to aim accurately, as the bird may rise or fall to E or F, though apparently flying direct for D when aim was first taken. A miss might then easily occur, as shown by the circle representing the spread of the shot at D.

FIG. V.—To obtain the correct line of flight, and allow for hesitation in pulling trigger, ignition of the powder, and passage of shot up the barrel, the first sight should be taken at G, or 8 ft. ahead of the bird; and the shooter should then instantly jerk his gun-muzzle forward as far again, or what appears as far again, and fire at H, and he will probably kill the pheasant.

Though, in order to be on the safe side, I have given 8 ft. ahead of the pheasant as an allowance for hesitation over the aim and other items of delay, I may say this is an outside estimate, save for a really slow marksman. Half as much, or a gun-length, would be sufficient for a fairly quick shot to allow between the bird and his *first* sight.

If the shooter, however, takes two sights, as I have recommended, he will aim much more accurately, but not so quickly, as if he took one aim, and fired the whole distance forward on putting his gun to the shoulder. If he acts the latter part, about 10 ft. ahead would be sufficient allowance for the bird from 35 to 40 yards, in the case of the man who does not dwell much on his trigger, and 12 ft. for the man who hesitates before firing his gun.

But the great difficulty when aiming ahead is to know what 8 ft. in the air forward of a crossing bird is, as there is nothing to suggest the distance.

What usually occurs to a young shooter when he aims in front of his game without any swing on his gun, and at the same time dwells on his trigger, and the best way for him to try and correct this sad state of affairs, is shown by the diagrams on page 154 and by the notes appended opposite thereto.

I have in these illustrations considered the shooter as striking his mark with the centre of his shot-circle, as if he fired a bullet at his game. He may, however, console himself with the fact that he does *not* fire an arrow or a bullet at the pheasant, but a large disc of shot some 4 ft. across, so that he has a considerable margin for inaccuracy. From the sketch given (fig. 6) it will be seen that, if the shooter fires a well-filled 30 in. circle of shot he can place his charge on all sides of his game at 40 yards, and yet kill it;[1] and that the actual killing-circle of his gun is, in consequence, a very wide one, and would almost include the four 30 in. circles shown in Fig. 6— that is to say, the hen pheasant depicted would be killed anywhere within this large area. For this reason we may, I believe, aim the same distance ahead

---

[1] The effect is very similar to that which occurs in making a cannon at billiards, for which purpose great accuracy is not necessarily required, as the result may be attained by the player's ball striking on either the right or left side of the ball that is played at.

at from 30 to 40 yards at a crossing bird—that is, if we shoot forward of our game at an imaginary point

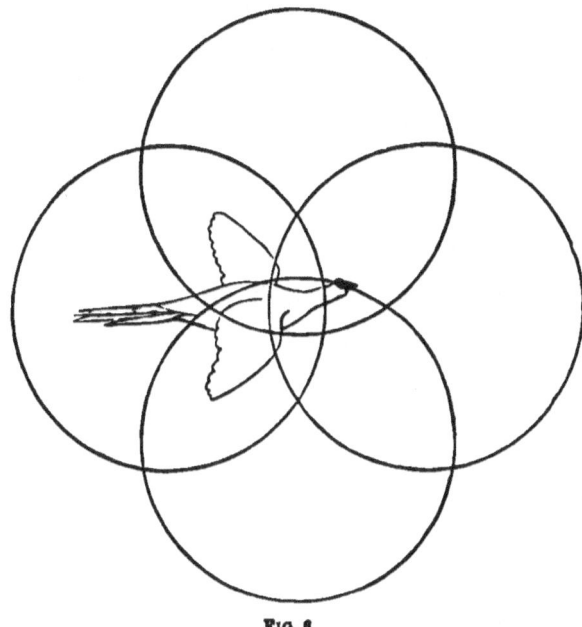

FIG. 6.

in the air, with a stationary gun at the moment of pulling trigger.

I will now say something on a subject which has always interested me very much, and which is, 'the lateral movement of a gun in the hands of a shooter, and the corresponding intervals at which the charge of shot will strike along a line parallel with the earth, as in the case of firing at an overhead bird or one crossing at right angles.' The earliest experiments of the kind I undertook were carried out by placing a gun on a pivot close to the ground, with a foot-rule under the barrels, and sighting the latter at a stick placed upright 40 yards distant. I then moved the sight laterally half an inch at a time, placing fresh sticks at right angles to the line of fire to mark the aim in each position. This gave me the divergence of the centre of the charge of shot at 40 yards, according to the lateral movement of the muzzle of the gun; and it was an easy matter to stretch strings from each mark to the first position of the sight of the gun, as when directed towards No. 1 stick, so that the intermediate measurements between the strings were easily ascertained, according to the displacement of the barrels from their original line of fire.

As I had doubts concerning the accuracy of my deductions, I consulted Mr. F. Toms, and he has most kindly worked out the annexed table for me from the records of experiments which have been published by Mr. R. W. S. Griffith; and the figures agree with my own calculations.

In these calculations the flight of the bird is stated to the nearest inch, and the movement of muzzle to the nearest tenth of an inch, in order to show the gradual variations; but for ordinary practical purposes it would suffice to consider the nearest foot in the one case, and the nearest inch in the other.

XII. ON CORRECT AIMING (THEORETICAL)

TIMES, VELOCITIES, &c., WITH 3 DR. AND 1 oz. OF No. 6.

Distance of bird	Time taken by shot in transit	Mean velocity of shot	Flight of bird, at 40 miles per hour, during transit of shot.	Lateral movement by the shooter of the muzzle of his gun
	sec.	feet per sec.	ft. in.	inches
15 yards	·0411	= 1095	2 5	2·4
20 ,,	·0568	= 1056	3 4	2·5
25 ,,	·0743	= 1009	4 4	2·6
30 ,,	·0932	= 966	5 6	2·7
35 ,,	·1146	= 916	6 9	2·9
40 ,,	·1377	= 872	8 1	3·0
45 ,,	·1625	= 831	9 6	3·2
50 ,,	·1909	= 786	11 2	3·4
55 ,,	·2231	= 740	13 1	3·6
60 ,,	·2614	= 689	15 4	3·8

N.B.—No time-allowance included for pull of trigger or passage of shot up the barrel.

TIMES, VELOCITIES, &c., WITH 3 DR. AND 1⅛ OZ. OF No. 6.

Distance of bird	Time taken by shot in transit	Mean velocity of shot	Flight of bird, at 40 miles per hour, during transit of shot	Lateral movement by the shooter of the muzzle of his gun
	sec.	feet per sec.	ft. in.	inches
15 yards	·0431	= 1044	2 6	2·5
20 ,,	·0596	= 1007	3 6	2·6
25 ,,	·0776	= 966	4 7	2·7
30 ,,	·0975	= 923	5 9	2·9
35 ,,	·1192	= 881	7 0	3·0
40 ,,	·1429	= 840	8 5	3·2
45 ,,	·1689	= 800	9 11	3·3
50 ,,	·1979	= 758	11 8	3·5
55 ,,	·2329	= 709	13 8	3·8
60 ,,	·2779	= 647	16 4	·4·1

N.B.—No time-allowance included for pull of trigger or passage of shot up the barrel.

Besides the relative velocities of shot and bird there are two other matters deserving consideration, though they are commonly overlooked. One is the time that elapses between the pulling of the trigger and the passage of the shot out of the muzzle of the gun; and the other is the amount of time taken by the shooter in the operation of pulling the trigger.

For ordinary purposes it will be near enough to say that the time occupied from the actual fall of the hammer to the shot quitting the muzzle is the hundredth part of a second; and in the hundredth part of a second a bird flying at the rate of 40 miles an hour would move just about 7 inches. Again, a man who has quick nerve-action also takes about the hundredth part of a second to pull the trigger *after* he has made the resolve to do so.[1] This means another 7 inches added to the distance the bird will have flown, or 14 inches in all, after the aim and intention to fire had been decided upon by the shooter.

Though a bird flying at 40 miles an hour, whether its distance from the gun is long or short, always moves this 14 inches during the pulling of the trigger and passage of the shot up the barrel, yet such a space requires no appreciable addition in the lateral motion of the muzzle by the shooter; for if he shoots *quickly* at first sight, he need only allow a forward space to his bird in relation to the time

---

[1] The particulars relative to the quickness or otherwise of nerve-action are derived from an article on 'The Physiology of Shooting,' by Dr. W. J. Fleming.

taken, according to distance, by the shot in travelling from the muzzle of the gun to the game.

I have alluded to the shooter who fires his gun without any hesitation, and pointed out the great advantage such a power gives him in regard to a forward aim. It is a very different affair, however, when a man hangs on his trigger, for *his* bird may fly several feet whilst he is converting thought into action.

There is a great difference in the quickness of touch in different persons, and its consequent effect on the allowance to be made in firing at crossing birds is very considerable. For instance, one man might pull the trigger in the hundredth part of a second, when other men would take longer times, varying from one to six hundredths of a second; consequently, though the bird might fly 7 inches only in the case of the quick man, it might move 3 to 4 feet in the case of the slow shooter.

From this we may see how easy it is for a slow, pottering marksman to miss crossing birds, unless he keeps the muzzle of his gun moving forward of his game till the shot is out of the barrel, as described in my previous letters on aiming. If the shooter, however slow he may be, can do *this*, the space the bird flies while the trigger is being pulled is eliminated, and all that takes effect is the time expended by the charge between the gun and the game.

A table of figures in relation to whether a shooter fires quickly or slowly is here given.

FLIGHT OF BIRD, AND LATERAL MOVEMENT OF MUZZLE, WHEN PULL OF TRIGGER IS QUICK AND WHEN SLOW.

(Charge, 3 dr. and 1⅛ oz. of No. 6; bird flying at 40 miles an hour.)

Quickest Pull of Trigger.

Distance of bird	Flight of bird during transit of shot	Lateral movement of gun-muzzle by the shooter
	ft. in.	inches
15 yards	3 8	3·7
20 ,,	4 8	3·5
25 ,,	5 8	3·4
30 ,,	6 11	3·4
35 ,,	8 2	3·5
40 ,,	9 7	3·6
45 ,,	11 1	3·7
50 ,,	12 9	3·8
55 ,,	14 10	4·0
60 ,,	17 6	4·3

Times included:
For pull of trigger . . . . . ·01 sec.
For passage of shot up the barrel . ·01 ,,
  ·02 sec.

Slowest Pull of Trigger.

Distance of bird	Flight of bird during transit of shot	Lateral movement of gun-muzzle by the shooter
	ft. in.	inches
15 yards	6 8	6·6
20 ,,	7 7	5·7
25 ,,	8 8	5·2
30 ,,	9 10	4·9
35 ,,	11 1	4·8
40 ,,	12 6	4·7
45 ,,	13 10	4·7
50 ,,	15 9	4·7
55 ,,	18 2	4·9
60 ,,	20 5	5·1

Times included:
For pull of trigger . . . . . ·06 sec.
For passage of shot up the barrel . ·01 ,,
  ·07 sec.

XII. ON CORRECT AIMING (THEORETICAL)

A curious point in connection with the very slow shooter (as may be seen by reference to the second column of the opposite table of figures) is, that instead of increasing his allowance for distant birds, he should reduce it, and give about 2 inches more lateral movement to his gun at 15 yards than he does at 40 or 50 yards. This apparent anomaly results from the fact that the effect of the lateral movement of the gun-muzzle gradually increases with the length of the radius—or, in other words, with the distance of the crossing bird that is fired at ; whereas the time taken in pulling the trigger is equal for all distances, and therefore its comparative influence diminishes with the increased distance of the bird, and the consequently longer time taken by the shot in reaching its destination.

Even in regard to the quick shooter, a similar deduction applies, but only to a very slight extent, as the lateral movement of the gun-muzzle in his case is practically about $3\frac{1}{2}$ in. for all distances from 15 to 50 yards.

The woodcut below represents a good flying shot made at a 'martin' (just as here drawn from the original arrow and bird) by my friend, Mr. G. Dunbar

Whatman, when a boy of twelve, and shows an accuracy of aim that he certainly now possesses with a gun in a remarkable degree, as I can testify from experience.

LETTER XIII

SOME REMARKS ON CORRECT AIMING, IN REGARD TO THE EYES

I WILL now say something about the 'eye question.' Everyone knows how often this subject has been discussed, and with what poor results. As I am not an oculist, I do not propose to enter into the scientific bearing of defective sight, but only to make a few observations relative to eyesight in a general way, as applicable to nine people out of ten. The gentleman who imagines that he is blessed, or the reverse, with such extraordinary vision as to see a pair of guns, in the act of aiming *quickly*, when he is handling one, and so forth, as some theorists try to persuade us is possible, must seek elsewhere for information.

When the subject of aiming is discussed among a party of shooters, inquiries are frequently made as to whether this or that sportsman aims with one eye or both.

For my part, I cannot see how it is even possible for a man with *ordinary* sight to *aim* with both eyes, even when his left eye *is* stronger than his right. Take, for example, a gun in your hands, and point it at a mark with both eyes open; you will find that your right eye is in reality the one that takes aim. Shut your right, and you will at once perceive it is impossible for your left eye to even look along the barrel, much less to align the sight; still, your left eye, in its way, should be as useful to you as your right when aiming at game, as I shall presently explain. No doubt the origin of shooting with one eye closed was from the constant custom, in days gone by, of firing only at animals sitting or at game flying straight from the shooter. When driving game came into fashion, the shooter soon discovered he had not then time to 'draw a bead' on his bird, and necessity in this case was again the mother of invention, and introduced the practice of shooting with both eyes open.

'My left eye is the stronger of the two,' exclaims a shooter.

'What does that matter, my good sir? Provided you suffer from no peculiarities of vision, you cannot aim with it under any conditions, unless you put your gun up to your left shoulder. As to one of your eyes being more powerful than the other, why there is not one man in a hundred whose eyes *are* of equal strength.'

If, for curiosity, you wish to discover which eye is the stronger, it is easily ascertained. Open a sheet of note-paper, lay a coin (such as a shilling) in the centre, trace the coin round with a pencil, and cut out the hole. Now hold the paper at arm's length fair in front of your face, and, with both eyes open, look at a mark (such as the face of a clock on the mantelpiece) through the hole. If, on closing the left eye, the hole cut in the paper jumps to the left, and you cannot see the mark through it with the right eye, the left is, of course, the eye that took the sight, and is the stronger one, as it overpowers the other; if this result is reversed, the right eye is the master. But how all this can affect aiming, when the aim is *forced* on the right eye, whether or no, whatever its comparative power may be, I do not realise.[1]

A man should say, 'I shoot with both eyes,' not 'I aim with both eyes,' if he wishes to convey that he keeps both his eyes open when taking aim.

The above is the simple and ordinary view of the question of aiming. The exceptional and more complicated one is as follows:—

About one shooter in thirty has unusual sight; such as when, with both eyes open, the left eye appropriates the aim and draws the muzzle of his gun to the left, whether the shooter is conscious of the

---

[1] A hole in a piece of paper is a far better test than a ring in any form: with the latter the eyes are apt to be confused through seeing other objects at the same time; with the paper this cannot occur.

fact or not. And it is generally the men thus circumstanced who cannot, for the life of them, make out what is wrong, and why; though they apparently take deadly aim, they do not drop their game as they feel they should do.

In such cases a good gunmaker will be of great assistance, and very likely vastly improve the shooting of such unlucky folk.

The first thing is to find out where the fault lies, and then to correct it by using a suitable gun, or adopting a system of aiming amenable to the peculiar vision in question. I will take a not uncommon case. We will suppose a gentleman who is not a good shot, and who yet is conscious he should often kill game when he does not, comes to his gunmaker for advice. I will in this instance place myself in the position of the gunmaker. Now, sir, stand opposite me across the room, open the breech of your gun, and look through the barrels just as a matter of form—a habit, by the way, that *every* shooter should acquire when aiming with a gun for the sake of experiment. You aim with your right eye, do you? Very well; keep both eyes open, and aim quickly at the small hole (the size of a sixpence, with a black rim round it) in the centre of the large sheet of paper I hold before my face. You bring up the gun true enough when aiming quickly, but I notice that, if you dwell on the aim, however slightly, you pull the sight slightly to your left, and doing this would often either put the shot off your game at 30 yards, or else cause you merely to feather it with the outside of the circle of the charge.

The fact is, by some complex arrangement of vision, not fully understood, your left eye draws the muzzle of the gun to the left, though you imagine your aim is true on the mark, and that you take a sight with your right eye.

This is the more puzzling to you because I notice, when you aim with speed, that you direct the barrels fair and true, your right eye being then forced to take aim. It is, however, when you dwell a trifle on the aim that your left becomes the master-eye and takes the lead, though it does not follow that it is the stronger eye of the two. You might shoot all your life and never discover this defect, for aiming at a mark will not assist you as will aiming at the eye of another person, who from practice can detect the slightest deflection in the direction of your gun-muzzle when pointed towards him. The only method by which sight like yours can be corrected is, either to close your left eye when aiming, and put it *hors de combat*; to shoot from the left shoulder; or to use a gun that, by the stock being much cast over from right to left, brings the barrels in line with your left eye.

I strongly advise the former plan, as a cross-eyed gun is an ungainly weapon to shoot with, and shooting from the left shoulder by no means easy to learn; and

XIII. EYESIGHT, AND ITS EFFECT ON THE AIM

you may console yourself with the fact that there are many very good shots who entirely close the left eye. Though a man who closes one eye may never be a really brilliant marksman, it is a great mistake to think he cannot be an excellent and steady shot. It is true various sporting authorities have lately discovered that a one-eyed shooter is *always* a slow, poking shot; but I cannot, for my part, agree with them, as I have known numbers of shooters who closed their left eyes to be quite the contrary.

I will not enter into the perplexing theory of seeing two objects when you aim—the real one, and one that appears like a shadow of it. It is always possible, *whatever* the sight may be, to see images *if you look long enough*, whether it be the muzzle of the gun, or your finger held before your nose; but I do not believe it is practicable, when taking a *quick* shot, to see a duplicate image of either the gun or the game, as there is not then *time* for such phantoms to appear.[1]

If a shooter wishes to test his sight, let him aim

---

[1] I have heard tell of a shooter who complained that when a single bird rose he saw two, and often fired at the wrong one; but I imagine that luncheon must have had something to do with such a lamentable state of affairs. A heavy luncheon is very detrimental to straight shooting—even the difference between a hot midday meal and a cold one has an influence sometimes on the way the birds come down to the guns in the afternoon. I do not for a moment intend to convey that liquid refreshments are to be blamed for this, but that a menu of puddings and pies, and strong cigars, perhaps in a hot room in a farmhouse, are quite sufficient to put a shooter off his aim at any time. I once heard a keeper remark, in reference to

quickly at a mark, with both eyes open, as I have directed him to do when trying the fit of his gun. Supposing the gun does fit him, and he covers the object with accuracy, then let him close his left eye, and notice if his aim is still fair and true with the right eye; if so, his sight is all that he need wish it to be. But if the shooter has doubts, let him ask a friend to test his sight for him, by means of a hole in a large piece of paper, in the manner I have explained; for though the shooter may readily discover for himself if a gun fits him, by observing if he is able to bring it accurately up to a mark time after time, still I am convinced that, when the question of eyesight as applied to aiming at game is concerned, no methods he can personally apply, should his vision be peculiar, will be of any real assistance to him in comparison with consulting a good gunmaker, as the latter can detect irregularities in aiming which the shooter cannot possibly see for himself.

ON SHOOTING WITH BOTH EYES OPEN

Shooting with both eyes open is a great advantage in many ways, as it enables a man to see on all sides at the moment of firing. Even in the act of pulling trigger a shooter can realise the presence of another bird or rabbit close to his left, or coming from that

this subject and the unnecessarily luxurious midday meal provided by a former employer, ' Oh ! Mr. —— would scarce miss a snipe in the morning, but he wouldn't "shoot a bull a-flying" in the afternoon.'

direction, and so fire his second barrel quicker than he could did he close his left eye on aiming, and as a result shut out all the parish on that side of his face from his view; he can, too, instantly notice if the effect of his first barrel was good, especially if the game was crossing to his left, and whether another shot is necessary; he can also sight his game a good deal quicker with both eyes open than if he merely used his right, which is principally employed in aiming, and apt to consider nothing for the moment but the part it is performing.

It may be said of the shooter who keeps both eyes open, that his right is employed in aiming the gun, while his left takes in the situation generally. No; it does not follow that the eyes are looking in different directions; it means the extent of vision is *doubled*, and the addition is a *very* useful and *safe* one too, in many ways.

I do not for a moment say a man who only utilises his right eye cannot be a good shot, for, as I have said, I know some *really good shots* who shut the left eye; but I advise a young shooter, *if* he can point his gun accurately with both eyes open, to keep them so while aiming, for reasons I have given. On the other hand, if he shuts his left eye, either from habit or necessity, let him bring his gun up to his game with both eyes open, and then close the left just at the instant of pulling trigger.

It is worth a shooter's while, in order to test his

sight, to take a few *easy* shots, *with both his eyes open*, at rabbits sitting. *If* he finds he can kill *these* shots with certainty, he may feel assured that, as far as shooting with both eyes open is concerned, he is all right, and that his success on winged game with a similar style of aiming is only a matter of practice and skill.

LETTER XIV

ON THE CARE AND CLEANING OF GUNS (THEIR LIABILITY TO DAMAGE, AND GENERAL SUPERVISION)

THERE are a good many sportsmen who, though they shoot in first-rate style, look upon a gun as merely a machine to kill with, that requires very ordinary care, and ought, with a little oil outside and a little tow at the end of a stick inside, to last in perfect condition for ever.

Though a gun may serve its owner well, and perhaps undergo an immensity of hardship, yet at night it has, I expect, sometimes to take its chance uncleaned, or, what is almost worse, is handed over, at the conclusion of a day's sport, to the tender mercies of an attendant, whose chief idea of cleaning a gun is to rub the barrels through a couple of times in careless fashion with a hard lump of powder-begrimed tow, and then smear them down outside with a damp and dirty cloth.

A gun that is in good order to start with can be kept so by a very simple application of cleaning materials; and provided it does not break down from sheer carelessness or rough usage, and obtains a wipe out every evening, and a thoroughly good cleaning inside and out at the end of each week, it should be in as perfect a state at the close of the season as it was at the commencement.

It is the laying a gun by without supervision for several days after it has been used that does the mischief. When a gun is in daily use, it will not suffer if the barrels obtain a fair amount of attention, as, whether one shot or a thousand be fired out of them, they do not hold in the latter case more residue than in the former.

A gun may keep in order for many years without repair if properly looked after, but it will go wrong at once if unfairly treated.

ON THE GENERAL TREATMENT OF A GUN WITH A VIEW TO ITS PRESERVATION

Putting on one side, however, for the present, the effect of actual neglect in the cleaning of a gun, there are many other ways in which it can be injured by those shooters who look upon it as an indestructible piece of goods.

I have heard a shooter remark: 'Oh! I never take any particular care of my gun, and yet it is just as good as when I bought it.' Is it, though? that is the question! How about those dents in the barrels, that crack in the handle of the stock, that bulge from a tight cleaning rod, that minute but serious indentation of the muzzle of one barrel or both, not to speak of the corrosion at the end of the powder-chamber and the pits in the barrels—all of which defects a gunmaker will point out in an instant, though their presence be totally unsuspected by the shooter; defects which cause his gun to be not quite such a sound and valuable weapon, or nearly such a good shooter, as its owner imagines it to be?

If you have good guns, send them to their maker for an overhaul at the end of every season. It will pay you well to do so, just as much as visiting that unpleasant but necessary gentleman the dentist once a year will, in the long run, serve you better than a visit every three or four.

I hear you say: 'If I take my guns to a gunmaker, he will want me to order a new pair.' If he did not make them, it is possible he may do so, as in the gun-trade no man seems to have a good word for a rival's handiwork; but if you take your guns to their manufacturer, he will have an interest in keeping them in good order and causing them to last as long as possible, as it is to his advantage to sell to the public guns that wear a long rather than a short time.

The shooter who really takes care of his gun is the man who is proud of it as an accessory to his sport. Such a man looks upon it as a friend, and grudges giving it the smallest blow or scratch outside, and keeps its barrels inside as smooth and bright as mirrors.

A man who treasures his gun will never apply the slightest force. If any of its parts do not fit, 'he will persuade their obstinacy to relax by coaxing rather than by pressure.' Undue pressure in putting a gun together, or taking it apart, means wear and tear; and *that* eventually leads to loose joints.

The young sportsman should never even allow the barrels to drop down with a jerk to their full extent when loading, as doing so causes unnecessary jar, to the detriment of the mechanism of his gun. He should ease the barrels down in his left hand when opening the breech, whether to load or unload.

All such little attentions to guns cause them to last far better than the weapons which are not so carefully treated.

For example, when a party of shooters are resting, or at luncheon, the careless will place their guns anyhow, and have little regard to their safety from damage. The **careful** shooter will seek hither and thither till he has found a snug corner for his gun, in which he is confident it cannot possibly come to harm. A gun is safer when laid on the ground than leaning against a wall, should dogs be about; I have seen a couple of quarrelling dogs send a row of guns clattering like ninepins down on the stones.

The muzzles of gun-barrels are easily bruised when rested against a wall; and as keepers and loaders are apt to descant on the merits of a number of guns, according as they favour their individual masters, while the latter are, perhaps, busily engaged in refreshment, the weapons may then be handled in anything but a gentle manner; and the clashing of two pairs of barrels, brought in violent contact by a couple of assistants swinging them about as they aim at imaginary game in the sky, is no unusual occurrence should the sportsmen be out of sight.

For my part, if I am obliged to lean a gun against a wall, I invariably pull a glove over the muzzle as a protection thereto, and as a capital plan to hinder it from slipping, as well as a gentle hint that the gun is not to be meddled with. Placing a gun in a cart or carriage without its being guarded by a strong case, with stock and barrels asunder, is also a sure way of injuring it sooner or later.

Guns are sometimes used in an extraordinary fashion. I have seen a shooter strike a dog with his gun, beat a bush for a rabbit with it, use it as an alpenstock when ascending a hill, push a boat from shore by pressing the muzzle against a quay; and it is a not *very* rare occurrence to see a shooter take his gun sideways and throw it across a ditch, to be caught —or not—by an assistant on the further bank!

Whether the sport enjoyed be rough and wild, as when seeking wildfowl, or the reverse, as in game-shooting, still a gun can be kept in equally good order with ordinary attention, for a little care bestowed on it to avoid rough usage, and a little cleaning inside and out *as required*, will keep it in proper condition as long as its stock and barrels hold together. A little neglect, and the gun has to be sent for repair, or, worse still, is irretrievably damaged.

The state of a gun outside will readily tell a critical observer how its owner treats it, and enable him to form a pretty correct opinion of its inside; for the shooter who is careful of the general appearance of his gun is certain to take good care of its important parts, though the latter are not so easy of inspection by his friends.

The stocks of some shooters' guns are scored all over from being dragged against thorns as their owners scramble through hedges; it is true this is but a matter of looks, but, as I have said, the man who is not careful of his gun in one way, is likely to neglect it in another and more serious respect.

THE BARRELS AND ACTION

The barrels of a gun really require the greatest supervision, for on these its actual usefulness depends; the locks and fittings, though they should not, of course, be disregarded, are but accessories of secondrate value in comparison with the barrels.

If a gun is in good order, nothing is better to

XIV. THE CARE AND CLEANING OF GUNS

keep it so than vaseline—it being the very best composition ever devised for this purpose; it may be rubbed on every part of the inside or outside of a gun, the locks included. Vaseline is also a splendid preservative for wood, making it pliable and waterproof.

When a gun is in daily use, be careful to avoid a surplus of lubricant, as, if there be an excess of oil left on, it will clog the mechanism of the gun and collect dust and grit—the presence of the latter being very detrimental to its wearing parts. If a gun has been out in the wet, it should be thoroughly dried with cloths in every part, finished off with an old silk handkerchief, and then brushed over lightly with vaseline.

Push some *clean* tow several times through the barrels of a gun after using it, then an old piece of soft cloth, and lastly some tow soaked in vaseline. The next morning, if the gun is to be used, rub out the vaseline; if the gun is to be laid by, clean again thoroughly with tow and cloth and finish with vaseline as before.

By putting vaseline on a gun at the end of a day's shooting any rust will be softened by the following morning, and can then easily be removed without all that elbow-grease that is often bestowed on a gun with a view of polishing it up over-night, and which, by the amount of friction given whilst grit and rust may be present, is no good thing for its fittings and barrels. In the care of his guns, the object of the shooter should be to keep them in such good order that they can be cleaned with *ease* instead of by *violent exercise.*

The action of a gun and its bolts and lumps are made to fit so close and air-tight that the less rubbing they get the longer will their parts fit without a shake, and as they did when the gun was new.

If possible, the action and working parts of a gun should never be cleaned save with a wad of tow, a soft cloth, or an old silk handkerchief; for rubbing and scrubbing their interstices and angles with a piece of stick, a wire brush, and (heaven preserve the gun!) with emery in any form, are methods always to be avoided. It is not that a piece of stick in itself could wear the fittings of a gun; it is the atoms of rust or grit that the application of the stick grinds, almost like sandcloth, against the metal-work.

THE LOCKS

The locks of a well-made gun are so completely sheltered from the atmosphere that they will keep clean and dry in the worst of weather, and should be as little interfered with as possible—a thin coat of vaseline over their flat surfaces, and touching their working parts very lightly with a fine, soft, paint-brush dipped in sweet oil once during the year, should be enough for them. If gun-locks are rusted, no amateur can possibly set them right again. He may, however, soak the affected parts in paraffin, and, after rubbing this off, scrub them in hot soap-and-water, and when quite dry apply a little sweet oil. By doing this they can be kept in order for a time; but where rust has once eaten in, it cannot be taken out properly except by a gunmaker, who will repolish the sore places.

Taking the locks of a gun off will eventually cause their accurate fit into the woodwork of the stock to suffer, and minute crevices will appear round the edges of the lock-plates, and water and air will be admitted, and rust be the result, though the said crevices would scarcely admit the point of a needle.

Round the edges of the metal-work is one of the first places where an inferior gun will fail, and show gaps, very often through the wood of the stock shrinking from improper seasoning, as well as from the lock-plates themselves, or the metal, being incorrectly fitted.

Vaseline, well rubbed in all round the lock-plates or edges of the metal-work of a gun will prevent the wood from swelling or shrinking; and, should there be a slight gap, it can be filled up with a little beeswax, so as to keep out the air and, hence, the moisture and rust that would otherwise surely percolate through the opening.

ON TAKING A GUN TO PIECES

Should it be necessary to take any part of a gun to pieces, act slowly and deliberately, taking care to have a couple of saucers handy, in which to place the screws as they are removed. Be careful to select screwdrivers of proper size; if used too large for the notches of the screws, the former will slip about over the metal of the gun and cause scratches, and every scratch will form a receptacle for rust, not to speak of its unsightliness. Be sure the screws are turned in again, when replaced, just the right distance, with their notches all level with the line of the barrels.

Before putting a screw back into its hole, rub it over with an old tooth-brush to clean its threads, afterwards with an oiled rag; and clean out the hole it fits into with a small twist of fine tow. And make it a golden rule *never* to force anything back into its place that sticks, for depend upon it it is not meant to do so; rather send the part to a gunmaker, as it will be cheaper to do this than to replace damages. This advice is especially applicable to a first-class gun, as in its case every screw and piece is so beautifully made and fitted that a breakage is a costly affair.

Here is a hint as to how to untwist a stubborn screw. First of all, see that your screwdriver fits well into the bottom of the notch of the screw in question; in case it does not, a file will soon make it. Having soaked some *paraffin* round the *head* of the screw, press the screwdriver well home, and, taking a stout pair of pincers, or, better still, a small wrench, seize the screwdriver just above where it enters the notch of the screw; then, by pressing on the handle of the former, and using the pincers as a lever, you will very likely start the screw. If this method fails, call in professional assistance.

Never put any part of a gun-lock in a vice without previously protecting it with a piece of soft, thick leather, doubled two or three times at least. Even with this precaution very few amateur artisans will avoid doing some slight injury to the parts held. Let me impress upon the young sportsman that he should not, on any account, place the *barrels* of his gun in a vice. A friend of mine once bought a vice for his gun-room, as he said it would be so convenient for holding a gun should any portion of it require unscrewing. I really believe that vice cost him eventually as much as a pair of new guns, owing to the damages resulting from its improper application. I do not believe that any sportsman's home is complete if it does not possess a workshop, or, at all events, some corner in which he can keep his tools in readiness for the many odd jobs that will be necessary in relation to his outfit of guns and rods, and other implements of sport; but at the same time I would advise him to *very* carefully feel his way before brandishing his tools about on such a fine piece of workmanship as a highclass gun.

As to keepers, nine out of ten are a rough-handed lot when they come to clean a gun, or take it to pieces;

and many of them seem to imagine that, because a gun is made of wood and iron, it is as strong as a field-piece.

Cleaning guns well and carefully should be an accomplishment as *much* a part of a keeper's *duty* as rearing his *game* or breaking his *dogs*.

For a shooter to use a costly gun all day, and then in the evening hand it over to the tender mercies of everybody or anybody to look after its interests, is almost as bad as if a hunting-man, on his return home after a run with the hounds, were to give up his horse to be groomed and fed by a careless or inexperienced stableman. Sooner than act the former part, I would take my guns upstairs and put them to bed till I could clean them myself; for 'twere better if a shooter's guns were well cleaned but twice a week by himself, than if carelessly attended to every evening by his attendant.

It is best for a shooter, should he not clean his guns himself, to give them into the charge of *one* servant only, with strict orders that no one else should even touch them; and remember, a case with lock and key will best enforce *that* precaution. The shooter should, of course, take care that his servant is well drilled concerning how to treat a gun, how to clean it, how to take it to pieces and coax it together again without using force, how to ease down its springs, how to lay it down safely and stand it up without chance of injury; and let it be remembered that, when not in actual use, a gun is *never* so safe or keeps better than when *locked* up in its leather case, its stocks and barrels apart.

A fine pair of guns are well worth looking after properly; and I really believe, if some shooters took as much care of their guns as they do of other articles costing some fifty times less—their umbrellas, for instance—the former would last just half as long again as they do.

If you have a servant to look after your guns, inspect the latter with a critical eye when taking them into your hands on the morning of a day's sport; for by your acting thus an assistant will realise that his master is ready to notice any delinquencies in the matter of rough usage or careless cleaning of guns, and he will probably bestow care on, and take pride in, their state of preservation in consequence.

PITS IN BARRELS

I have described how easy it is to keep a gun properly when it is in a *good state to start with*; but it is the gun that has suffered by *neglect* that is so difficult to keep in order.

Recollect that *damp* and *wet* are the most insidious and dangerous enemies that guns have to contend with. If a gun could be kept absolutely dry after being *thoroughly* cleaned, it would never rust, provided it had never shown symptoms of rust in its past history; therefore, the nearer we can approach this state of safety from rust the longer will our guns retain their good condition.

The barrels of an unused gun are so hard and smooth inside that there are no irregularities, however minute, for rust and dirt to adhere to; but once a gun has been shot with, even but a score times, this bright, mirror-like surface becomes tarnished and imperceptibly made rough by the action of the powder and shot; then, if unchecked, rust and dirt will find a natural lodgment in the barrels, the bad effects of which are unnoticeable at first, but evident enough in course of time.

It is the little ' sores '—I can use no better word —known as ' pits' that ruin the barrels; and I need hardly point out that the barrels of a gun are its most important parts. Its other belongings can be renovated piecemeal, and the gun be as good as ever. Not so in regard to its barrels. These will have to be replaced entire if much damaged; and, in the case of a good gun, a precious costly job will their renewal be.

The ' pits' that form in a barrel, though they begin but as minute specks, which could *then* easily be rubbed out, result from neglect and carelessness in cleaning, and are a special punishment for leaving a gun unexamined when laid aside out of use.

If a young shooter values his gun, he should watch for the appearance of the small specks that are *certain* to appear in course of time in his gun-barrels, and out with them at once with a brass wire brush and plenty of subsequent cleaning. These specks will *surely* blossom into ' pits ' *if* disregarded, and are then real cankers in the life of the gun.

'Pits,' when shallow, as in their early stage, can be bored out by the gunmaker; but when pretty deep— and they are not generally discovered *before* they represent *serious* mischief—there is no getting rid of them. They will, *nolens volens*, go from bad to worse; and though with their presence the gun may be perfectly safe for many seasons, or may reach a dangerous stage in a short time, it will never *shoot* properly again.

When once these abominable ' pits '—in fact, holes —have formed, they will always retain moisture in their cavities. You may rub and scrub, and oil and wash for a week, but you won't get rid of the moisture at the bottom of the 'pits'; there it will remain in spite of all your efforts: for your brushes and cloths will all pass *over*, not *into*, them, and probably fill them with moisture at the very time you are employed in cleaning the barrels; and, do what you will, these pits will ever be traps for holding the very concomitants that you are most anxious to dislodge from your barrels.

To refer to the dentist once more. He can fill a hollow tooth for you, after first cleaning out the cavity: and could *you* fill up the ' pits ' in your gun-barrels in a similar way, all would be well; but, as it is, you cannot do so, and the injury caused by their presence will steadily increase.

I will not enter into the chemical causes that bring these 'pits' into existence; it is sufficient to know they do come, and quickly enough, too, if common care be not taken to keep them in check, whether a chemical or a black powder be used, though the former compound does not injure the barrels of a gun that is neglected so quickly as the latter.

LETTER XV

THE CARE AND CLEANING OF GUNS
(*continued*)

HOW TO PRESERVE A GUN IN GOOD ORDER, AND HOW TO PREVENT A GUN IN BAD CONDITION FROM BECOMING STILL WORSE

DURING the last few seasons, when wildfowling on salt water, I have kept my big and small duck-guns in beautiful order by applying a plentiful allowance of thickly-mixed boiling water and soap. It struck me if I could keep guns at sea[1]—the severest trial they can undergo—in proper trim by such simple means, there was no reason why I should not treat my game-guns in the same way; and the result has amply repaid the experiment. Yet, simple and effective as

---

[1] Raw linseed oil is rare stuff to smear over guns when at sea; and mercurial ointment brushed over game-guns before putting them on one side after the shooting season will keep them in a good state for at least a couple of months. In fact, *anything*, whether it be in the shape of oil, tallow, grease, varnish or lard, that will form a waterproof skin or coating between the *metal* and the *atmosphere*, will shut out rust from attacking the gun.

this treatment is, it is one I have rarely seen practised.

On the face of it, it appears so easy to clean breechloaders, that I really believe this supposition accounts a good deal for the way they are neglected.[1]

The use of hot water and soap has not the effect of cleaning the barrels merely as a 'washing mixture,' as the strongest recommendation for this application is that the properties of the soap eradicate the harmful acids left in the barrel by the combustion of the powder—acids which a flood of oil would not remove.

When you see by the presence of 'specks,' or even feel conscious your gun-barrels *ought* to require a downright good cleaning, give them hot water and soapsuds, and a scrub through with a *brass* wire brush, finishing off with clean hot water and pieces of flannel; and when the barrels are quite dry, though still warm to the touch, rub in a light coat of vaseline, which can be rubbed out again before next using the gun.

Keep a score pieces of *coarse*-textured flannel for cleaning purposes, some 3 in. or 4 in. square, with a small hole in the centre of each, so that they can be strung on a piece of wire when not in use; they can

---

[1] Before the era of breechloading guns, muzzle-loaders were usually cleaned by the use of hot or cold water and soap. For the sake of curiosity, I the other day removed the screw-plugs of several old flint-guns I possess, and, on my word, the barrels were in a better condition than those of many a modern gun I have seen.

be washed as necessary. One-half of these pieces of flannel can be applied to the dirty part of a gun's cleaning, and the other half for finishing off with. The best stick to use for this purpose I give an illustration of. Such a one has nothing about it that can possibly injure the barrels.

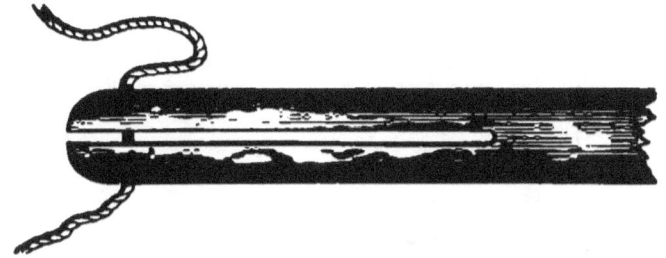

End of cleaning-rod for a 12-bore gun (full size). By tying the string of the stick tight, after placing in the slit a piece of flannel, the material will not move.

End of cleaning-rod (reduced), showing flannel in position for cleaning a gun.

When washing barrels out, use a piece of wood, with two upright, quadrangular projections on it (see next page); then the soap-and-water will pass freely up the barrels as you wash them, with their muzzle-ends downwards, in a pail. All this may seem as if it entailed a lot of trouble; but the trouble is little in comparison to making a gun last in as good order for a score years as when new; and it is for the young shooter who wishes to keep his gun in such good condition that I have set down these details.

The application of the brass wire brush, with the aid of soap-and-water, is the *only* method I know

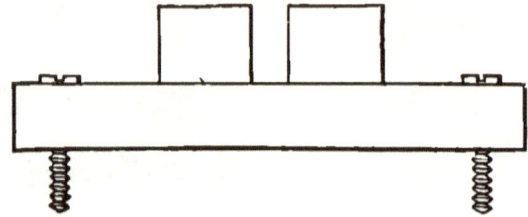

To be screwed to a piece of round wood 6 in. in diameter.

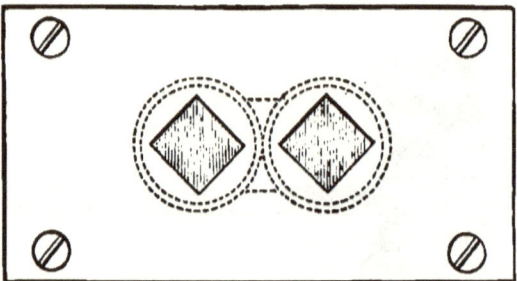

The dotted lines show outline of barrels (reduced) when in position for cleaning.

that will *really* remove specks, dirt, rust, and lead from the barrels of a gun in *bad* condition. In the case of a gun in *good* order, turpentine will loosen the lead that is smeared inside the barrels, and which a cloth would pass over, or but partially efface; but this liquid, being very sticky, must not on any account be rubbed on the working parts of a gun. To remove the lead from a barrel that is new, or bright and smooth from being in good order, is an easy matter compared with taking it out of one which through neglect has become rough and 'pitted' inside.

If the barrels of a gun are in a bad state of dirt, give them in the first place a swab out with *cold water*, and the use of the wire-brush at the same time; afterwards repeat with boiling water and soap, and finish with clean boiling water. By acting thus you can make a gun in *very* bad order as clean as it *can* be made. The cold water will, with the friction of the brush, have an effect in loosening dirt that the hot will only soften; and though cold water cannot really clean the barrels, it will prepare them for the final operation of hot water and soap—the latter being the only treatment that will partly check the acids of the powder from further damaging barrels that are pitted already, and will also, if applied now and then during the season, *prevent* these pits from forming *at all*.

A couple of nail-brushes and two or three toothbrushes, kept especially for removing (with the aid of hot water and soap when necessary) any obdurate patches of rust from the outside of a gun, or the working parts of the action, will be found *most useful*. The brushes should not be used with much oil, or they will become too clogged to be of service.

Though a gun should never require paraffin, if

kept in fair condition, it is well for the shooter to know that paraffin put on a gun, inside and out, for a few hours, or at most a night, and then rubbed off with a cloth, is the best way to remove a slight amount of rust; but if paraffin is left on a gun with the intention of preventing rust, it will have a contrary effect, as this oil contains so much water that after a time rust will form wherever the paraffin has been applied to the metal.

SOME CONCLUDING REMARKS ON CLEANING A GUN

To retain a gun in good order when put aside for some time without attention, treat the barrels with hot water and soap as I have described, and then cover the gun (lock, stock, and barrels) with refined neatsfoot oil—by refined I mean that all the water has been taken out of the oil. Neatsfoot, though nasty to handle, is capital stuff to put on a gun, and is a most useful and successful preservative.

I have kept guns in fine order at sea, when not in everyday use, by merely filling their barrels with clean tow that had, in order to perfectly dry it, been previously heated before a fire inside a tin; the damp is then absorbed by the tow, and prevented from settling on the metal of the barrels.

When cleaning a gun, be *very* jealous of any sediment or moisture lurking in the end of the cartridge-chamber; never omit to clean this part very thoroughly—it is the most vital part of the barrels. A wire-brush attached to a short handle, the latter some 8 in. long, with a knob to lay hold of, to prevent the brush going too far up the barrels, will be found a convenient dodge for this particular purpose.

Do not forget, whilst cleaning a gun, to rub the faces and angles of the breech, and *all* the parts that work in one with another, with an oiled rag, to remove grit, as the presence of the latter soon causes loose joints, and is particularly liable to accumulate about a gun on windy days when the soil is dry and sandy.

If your gun is in a sticky, dirty state after being laid by for some time, from the excess of lubricant put on for its preservation, you will find nothing equal to petroleum for removing the clogged oil, and polishing the gun up again ready for use.

Before quitting this subject of cleaning, I will say that, previous to the application of vaseline, a gun's barrels should be so clean and dry inside that a fine cambric handkerchief can be passed through them without the symptom of a stain; and I will add, that a large silk handkerchief heated before the fire is the very best thing to pull through a barrel *after* it has been cleaned and dried, to remove the least remnant of moisture, and to give the surface that brilliant *polish* inside which is the only *real* antidote to *rust*.

THE WIRE-BRUSH

I now give a hint on cleaning a barrel with the wire-brush. In nine cases out of ten, when this brush is applied to the gun, the operator pushes it in through the chamber of the barrel, and, holding the handle of the cleaning-rod, works the brush up and down inside, entirely ignoring the fact that, instead of *removing* the powder-scale, or rust, he is merely *smearing* it all over the interior of the barrel. The proper method is to place the handle-end of the cleaning-rod in first, and draw the brush after it out at the muzzle, as the latter is held downwards—*then* the dirt is really removed; yet how seldom is a barrel thus treated! Nothing equals a rub through with the wire-brush when a gun is not in use, as the brush will break up at once any specks or rust that adhere to the metal. Though cloth and tow will polish and cause a barrel to *look* clean, neither will really eradicate specks of rust. A brass wire-brush cannot possibly score the inside of a barrel—you might as well endeavour to scratch glass with the thumb-nail. A *steel* brush will *in time* score the surface of a barrel, and has the disadvantage that, now and then, small pieces of the wire snap off, and when they drop by chance into the action of the gun are quite capable of causing loose joints and other damage.

A wire-brush should be of large size—those usually sold by gunmakers are not of much use; and I give below a full-scale drawing of what I have found the most suitable form, and one which will

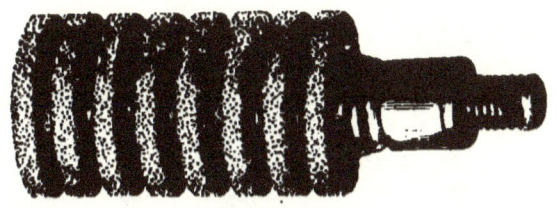

FIG. 21.

Brass-wire scratch-brush for 12-bore gun. Full size. N.B.—When the brush becomes foul, hold it over the flame of a lamp or candle for a few seconds, and it will be effectually cleaned.

clean out a barrel thoroughly and quickly. Messrs. Pape, gunmakers, Newcastle-on-Tyne, make these brushes for me as well as can be desired, both strong and lasting.[1]

[1] Here is a useful dodge to assist you to clean your gun when away from home. Carry in your gun-case, in a small water-tight box, a piece of sponge, previously soaked in rangoon or other oil. You can then 'dab' the oil on your gun as required, and you can keep sufficient lubricant on a piece of sponge no larger than a small apple to last a season!

LETTER XVI

ON THE LOADING OF GAME-GUNS—POWDER

BLACK POWDER AND NITRO-COMPOUNDS

POWDER is naturally a subject of great interest to shooters. The ordinary black powder, such as No. 4, has been proved to kill as well as any chemical compound, but the amount of smoke that results from its combustion is a decided drawback to its use.

I have often seen shooters on a calm day, in a grouse-box, or when firing in covert, so enveloped in the smoke caused by black powder that it was impossible for them to see to aim successfully—in the first case, till the smoke had settled; in the second, till they had walked clear of it!

In the event of driven game, it is a *great* gain to use the smokeless powder, as it does not intercept the aim of the shooter, after he has fired, in regard to other birds approaching him. The serious disadvantage of black powder is that, in calm weather, under *all* conditions of shooting, it is liable to conceal the effect of the first barrel, if game has been wounded and ought to receive another shot.[1] The smoke from black powder will also frequently hinder a shooter from firing his second barrel quickly, should a couple or several birds rise together; and when the smoke hangs in a cloud, its presence certainly makes *driven* game suspicious of danger, and turns it from passing within shot of the man who uses this powder in his gun, to the benefit of those sportsmen present who chance to burn a nitro-compound.

The report of black powder is another drawback, especially on a small estate, for the loud, earth-quaking, long-drawn-out concussion it causes will start game running, when the short, sharp, rifle-like crack of a nitro-compound will have but little effect. I have frequently noticed this fact when posted at the end of a covert; and the difference between the way in which hares, and, late in the season, cock pheasants, will break out when the shooters are using the noisier powder, is very noticeable. As an instance, I may state that I often shoot wood-pigeons with ' Schultze' only a few hundred yards distant from my duck-decoy; whilst if I fire a few shots with the black powder, as I have done for experiment, off go the wild ducks at once. I must not, however, deny to the

---

[1] You can almost fancy you see your shot strike when using a nitro-compound; at all events, you can see the feathers fluff off your bird when it is struck, which is pretty nearly the same thing—an occurrence very likely to give you some useful information as to where the charge of shot strikes—hints that the smoke resulting from black powder would conceal from view.

black powder the advantages it *does* possess—no small ones either. It is very even and reliable in its shooting, and hence gives a more regular spread to the shot than its chemical rivals, though not as a rule such a close pattern; it is very safe—certainly more so than EC or Schultze;[1] and it is also practically free from deterioration by age or climatic influences.

Though it is a fact that the nitro-compounds have less recoil and, strange to relate, burn more slowly than the black powder, I do not find these advantages are noticeable so far as the effect on the shooter is concerned if a *number* of shots be fired, as the sharp crack which results from the explosion of a chemical compound is in such case just as liable to cause headache as the combustion of the black grain; and, after firing, on many occasions, from 500 to 600 cartridges in a day at game with black and chemical powders, I am confident that a charge of 82 gr. of Messrs. Curtis &

---

[1] Some of the most notable marksmen in our islands use black powder. Lord de Grey informs me that he invariably shoots with Curtis & Harvey's Diamond Grain No. 2, and adds, that he is confident that no nitro-compound ever shot as well as the best fine black powder, and that he has converted many of his friends to the same views. As Lord de Grey's excellence as a game-shot and experience of the gun is unsurpassed, this supposition on his part carries great weight. I will add, it is a well-proved fact that a fine powder *does* shoot harder, and, of course, kill *farther*, than the usual grain, as No. 4; but at the same time it causes a considerable increase of recoil, and strain to the gun, though it has an advantage, in the matter of smoke, over a coarser grain, for, the coarser the powder, if black be used, the more the smoke and—dirt!

Harvey's No. 4 does not jar one's system to a greater extent than 42 gr. of Schultze or EC.[1, 2]

Our trusty old friend the black powder has gone much out of fashion since the introduction of Schultze and EC; yet its only *real* disadvantage—though *certainly* a *serious* one to the shooter—is its excessive production of smoke as compared with its chemical rivals.

The great advantage of a chemical compound is the power it gives the shooter of taking a second shot,

---

[1] *Gun Headache.*—On this troublesome annoyance, the most distressing *penalty* a shooter has to undergo, I consulted Dr. Quain; for I was aware that, besides being famous in his *profession*, he had a long and varied experience in *shooting*. Dr. Quain very kindly explained to me his suppositions on the subject, and wrote: 'There are a certain class of nerves which are intimately associated with the digestive organs, and are *also* intimately associated with the circulation of the brain, and when digestion is taking place these nerves are very susceptible to a shock (such as the firing of a gun), and therefore through them the circulation of the brain may be disturbed.' Dr. Quain added that 'it is possible after a "heavy luncheon"'; the nerves he alludes to are particularly affected by an unusual shock, not only during the digestive process, but subsequently, and 'the remedy would seem to be, Take care of the digestive functions, avoid overexcitement, and *watch the circumstances that* appear to produce "gun headache," *and avoid the causes.*'

[2] I have met more shooters suffering from gun headache since the nitro-compounds came so much into fashion than was the case previously. Nitro-compounds are nothing but dynamite! The latter is their *real* description; and it is worthy of remark that all artisans who work in dynamite are cautioned against handling or smelling this explosive more than is absolutely necessary, as being very liable to cause *severe headache*! However here is *my* idea of gun headache framed in simple language :—

Many good things \
Much smoking } = { Gun headache, \
Sitting up late at night / Bad marksmanship, and \
Loss of temper.

or, if necessary, of firing a succession of quick shots, through the absence of any noticeable smoke.

As to safety, nothing can be safer than the black powder; yet I am bound to admit that, during the past half-dozen years I have fired over 60,000 cartridges loaded with Schultze without misadventure; though I have nevertheless had, I believe, three or four out of that number that, for some reason, nearly sent my gun flying out of my hands from excessive recoil, and seemed to loosen all the teeth in my head. If, however, a shooter obtains his cartridges from a *reliable* firm of gunmakers, and is careful his powder is not kept at too high a temperature, he is quite safe with Schultze or EC. But I would advise the sportsman who cannot answer favourably on such points as these to use black powder, as then no accident is ever likely to occur, save from some defect in his gun.

It is that one cartridge in, perhaps, several thousand, that explodes with a crash, which with a nitro-compound is to be dreaded, and gives such a disagreeable reminiscence for many days, and at the time makes you feel as if you had been blown up—a feeling that, if you are using an *inferior* gun may be more *real* than *imaginary*.

Personally, I prefer a nitro-compound—Schultze for choice—as I find from experience the latter has within the last couple of years become very reliable, though in reality there is but little to choose between it and EC for general excellence; and I am willing to risk an occasional cartridge that kicks like a horse, rather than give up the advantage of burning a powder almost devoid of smoke—a great boon, and one that is not enjoyed at intervals, on rare occasions, but *continually*, and in *almost* every shot that is fired from the beginning to the end of a day's shooting. At the same time, I take good care my cartridges are thrown away when wet, to avoid any risk of their being over-dried through some kindly officious person roasting them on the hob at home! I also see they are not kept in too warm a room, and are removed from my gun at the close of a drive, or at the finish of a hot corner, as leaving cartridges loaded with a chemical powder in the barrels, when the latter are in a heated condition, is *just* as *injudicious* as placing them too near a *fire*.

Black powder requires no supervision other than preserving it from damp; and, should it suffer from this cause, it can be easily dried without risk, and almost at any temperature. On the other hand, putting on one side the danger of over-heating, a *slight*, and usually quite *unsuspected*, degree of damp *ruins* the *efficiency* of nitro-compounds, as, in spite of the improvements of late years in waterproofing them, they are still materially affected by damp—far more so than is the case with black powder.

Nitro-compound cartridges that have merely been out on a damp day are liable to become weak and irregular in their shooting unless carefully dried for future use. As a shooter cannot at all times watch his cartridges, he should be most cautious that some blundering assistant does not take upon himself to dry a few before a hot fire, should they be wet, as then may come, in the case of nitro-compounds, the terrific recoil that will cause their strongest advocates to eschew them for ever.[1]

In the case of a *good, safe* gun, there is no powder so pleasant to use or easy to kill with as Schultze or EC; and it is worthy of note, that the unpleasant habit these powders sometimes have of filling the eyes with particles that cause one's optics to smart and

---

[1] There are other causes besides over-heating that result in excessive recoil, such as the use of too powerful caps by the cartridge-case maker, or the addition of a priming of fine black powder, or excessive compression in the turning down of the cases by the person who loads the cartridges. These details regarding safety are, however, the business of the manufacturer rather than of the shooter, and the latter, if he procures his cases from experienced dealers, may feel satisfied they are right enough in their contents *when delivered*. The EC cartridges supplied by Mr. C. Lancaster, and the Schultze by Messrs. Cogswell & Harrison—both of Old Bond Street—are particularly good in every way; and there is no doubt some firms, such as those I name, have acquired a specialty in turning out superior cartridges, and are deservedly patronised in consequence. Beyond doubt, *all* nitro-compounds require some care in loading, and differ materially in the way they should be treated. For instance, the EC requires a good amount of pressure to develop its force, and JB wants more pressure than EC; but Schultze's is virtually 'killed' when caked by excessive pressure. As to black powder, there is no difficulty of any kind in connection with loading cartridges with it.

blink just, perhaps, when game is flying thickest, is merely the result of imperfect combustion caused by improper loading. The other chemical powders are, in my opinion, not to be named with these two.

The most suitable black powders, in my experience, are No. 4, and Curtis & Harvey's medium grain, the latter size being between No. 3 and No. 4. They are both admirably adapted for use in game-guns, in regard to hard hitting, even strength, and *regular pattern* — the latter quality a *very* necessary one in a gun, and which black powder possesses to a greater degree than *any* chemical compound. At the same time, I strongly recommend the shooter to use Schultze or EC on all occasions, *if* his gun is a reliable one, *if* he can ensure his cartridges being properly loaded, and *if* he can depend upon them being kept at a correct temperature; and I will add, that a shooter should *often* seek *nearer home* than he imagines possible for the cause of weak force or excessive recoil in his nitro-compound cartridges, instead of at once laying the blame on his gunmaker.

LETTER XVII

ON THE LOADING OF GUNS—SHOT

GENERAL REMARKS ON SHOT—SOFT *v.* HARD SHOT, AND THE GLANCING OF SHOT—ON LOADING FOR LONG SHOTS—RECOIL

In the matter of shot there is not much to puzzle the shooter. Nos. 5 and 6—the latter for preference—are the usual and correct sizes to use on game. Anything smaller, such as No. 7, is best adapted for a small-bore, such as a 20. Sizes such as 8 or 9 are suitable for snipe-shooting only, and a larger size than 5 for wildfowl; and then only in a wider bore than a No. 12.

Taking into consideration all-round shooting in the British Islands, there is far more game killed with No. 6 than with any other size, as the experience of a large majority of sportsmen and experimentalists has proved that No 6 is, for general shooting and the average marksman, the most suitable in every way, not omitting the requirements of the gun itself.

No. 6 gives such a good pattern that, if a gun be held fairly straight, no game can escape being killed within a sporting distance. It has also ample penetrative power, and $1\frac{1}{8}$ oz. of No. 6 from a good

No. 12 cylinder-gun, and $1\frac{1}{16}$ oz. from a medium choke, should drop game dead up to 40 yards, and, under certain conditions—as in the case of crossing shots—even farther. An ounce only of No. 6 contains enough pellets to kill with equal certainty from a full-choked gun, *if* the shooter can aim with sufficient accuracy to enable him to strike his game with the concentrated pattern thrown by a choked barrel.

No. 5 is a heavier shot, and, pellet for pellet, would kill farther than No. 6; but as it contains fifty-two pellets less to the ounce than No. 6, it of course gives a more scattered pattern. Theoretically, one pellet of No. 5 would, or, rather, *might* kill a bird when a pellet of No. 6 might not; but then a bird could easily be struck by four or five pellets of No. 6 when, perhaps, not more than three of No. 5 would do so, and the aggregate force of the blow given by the former size would then disable it as effectively as would the fewer, though heavier, pellets of the latter. So that there is not, I believe, any real difference in effect between the two sizes at the *average* distance game is fired at.[1]

But *if* we *can* put several pellets of No. 5 into the mark at a *long* range—sufficient, that is, to kill—*then* this shot, from its superior weight and penetration, would in such case certainly drop the game cleaner

---

[1] When I write that No. 5 will kill as well as No. 6, it should be understood I refer to the effect only of the shot itself on the game, without considering, as I afterwards do, which size is best for the shooter to use in regard to striking his mark.

than No. 6; but, save with a full-choked barrel, this cannot be regularly done: and I have in a former letter pointed out the disadvantage of a full-choke and the drawbacks attending its use.[1]

It is *only when* we can place an ample number of pellets of No. 5 shot into our game, so as to kill it with certainty—as, for instance, at rabbits, or at driven grouse or partridges, or close-lying birds—that I consider No. 5 is a superior shot to No. 6 to use in a cylinder-gun.

Depend upon it, the most deadly charge of lead for an average, or even a good shot to use, from ordinary 12-bore game-guns, that make patterns of from 130 to 150, is $1\frac{1}{8}$ to $1\frac{1}{16}$ oz. respectively of No. 6 shot (270 pellets to the ounce).

A perfect charge for a medium-choked 12-bore gun is $3\frac{1}{16}$ dr. of black or 42 gr. of chemical powder and $1\frac{1}{16}$ oz. of No. 6 shot.

With a cylinder-gun, $3\frac{1}{16}$ to $3\frac{1}{8}$ dr. of black or 43 gr. of a chemical powder and $1\frac{1}{8}$ oz. of No. 6 shot will kill game at any distance a 12-bore should be fired at.

---

[1] Lord de Grey uses No. 5 shot in full-choked guns. The small pattern that results from this combination in no degree handicaps such a deadly marksman, but, instead, gives him increased power of killing his game—an advantage in no way likely to be enjoyed, however, by an average good shot.

XVII.   ON THE LOADING OF GUNS—SHOT   209

From a full-choked gun, in the hands of a *first-class* shot, 1 oz. of No. 5 with $3\frac{1}{8}$ dr. of powder will kill splendidly, as this charge has more penetration than $1\frac{1}{8}$ oz., or than 1 oz. of No. 6, but is not, of course, nearly so easy to hit with, as the shooter will have to strike his mark with a shot-circle of narrow width, which, of course, implies *very* accurate aiming.

A gun must, however, be bored and regulated to shoot 1 oz. of shot with a regular pattern; a gun built for $1\frac{1}{8}$ oz. will, likely enough, not do so.

It is a not unusual custom for shooters to vary the loads in their guns. This is an error; for a good gun is regulated with great care to shoot a certain charge, which, in a 12-bore, is generally 3 dr. or $3\frac{1}{8}$ dr. of powder and $1\frac{1}{8}$ oz. of No. 6 shot.

Putting on one side the effect on the performance of a gun by using in it charges for which it was not intended, the substitution of one size of shot for another is only worth considering when one kind of bird or ground game is likely to be met with for an entire day (a somewhat rare occurrence); and carrying several batches of differently-loaded cartridges in separate pockets or bags is certain to cause confusion and annoyance, and is a terrible bore in the field as well. Rabbits may, however, be treated exceptionally, and $2\frac{3}{4}$ dr. of black or 38 gr. of a chemical powder

P

and ⅞ to 1oz. of No. 5 shot will do for them, even with a cylinder-gun.

For ordinary all-round sport with a cylinder or a medium-choked gun I strongly recommend the young shooter to adhere to No. 6 shot throughout the season. When once a shooter has acquired a successful system of loading his cartridges to suit his gun and himself, the less should he be inclined to change and experimentalise.

If a shooter invariably fired at pheasants, I should advise him to use a gun bored for No. 5 shot. If partridges and grouse were his only game, and he habitually walked for them, No. 6 would be his best size; for as these are comparatively small birds, plenty of pellets are required in the charge—that is, if they are to receive their proper allowance when they offer shots at over ordinary ranges. On the other hand, pheasants present a larger target, and a charge of No 5 will generally put plenty of pellets on the mark to kill, if the aim be correct; and a pheasant can now and then be brought down at a farther range with No. 5 than with No. 6. For rabbits, No. 5 is the best size, as rabbits are usually killed at a moderate range, and No. 5 will not, in such case, smother them with pellets to the same extent as No. 6; and what I have written about the rabbit equally applies to driven grouse, as well as driven partridges. For hares, there is no doubt No. 5, or even No. 4, is the killing-size.

However, as we cannot pull out of our pocket a cartridge loaded for hares, another for partridges, and a third for pheasants, according as each variety presents itself to our aim, we make a compromise, and that is to use No. 6 shot; and there is no doubt this size will kill in good style everything in the form of game in our islands, rabbits, hares, and wild duck included.[1]

CHILLED *v.* SOFT SHOT

Chilled shot is now in general use, as it is of better construction than when first introduced.

There is an impression, however, among sportsmen that chilled shot ricochets more than soft, and is therefore more likely to cause accidents—a theory uncommonly hard to prove. For my part, after making many experiments, I cannot discover that there is the least difference between the two in this respect, and I have fired at all sorts of objects, stone, iron, and wood, with paper placed at all angles near to receive the pellets. I find the soft and the hard will both glance at equally acute angles, and are just as ready, one or the other, to glance off a hard, or even, at times, a soft substance, if they strike it with

---

[1] For some seasons a fit of experimenting seized hold of me, and I carried all sorts of cartridges for all kinds of game; and this usually ended in my having to use up the loads intended for early partridges on pheasants, and those intended for ducks on early partridges of the following season.

the necessary inclination, and I imagine a pellet in the face from either size would be equally disagreeable.¹

The irregular pellets found in game, whether hard or soft shot be used, result from the shot being crushed out of shape through the violent hustling it undergoes in the barrel on the charge being fired; and it is generally imagined that the considerable percentage of every charge that diverges from the true line of flight, and travels wide both of game and target, consists of the more misshapen pellets, which, from their loss of a spherical form, fly in eccentric directions.

This is a puzzling question; and it is a matter for conjecture how it is we find so many irregular pellets in game if, as imagined by theorists, the damaged ones cannot travel in a straight line to the mark aimed at. That the shot does not become irregular from contact with the game, is proved by the many dents and faces that appear all over the former instead of its being merely flattened on one side.

I am of opinion that the accuracy of the flight of shot is not, practically speaking, affected by its being crushed out of its spherical shape inside the barrel of the gun, and that the pellets which diverge most, and do not travel within 3 ft. or 4 ft. of the

---

¹ I recollect a sportsman entering the shop of a well-known gunmaker, and inveighing in strong terms against the use of chilled shot as being dangerous, and finally declaring he would never use it again. 'Sir,' said the gunmaker, 'you must bear in mind that will not prevent *your friends using it.*'

object aimed at, have their direction changed by contact with the bulk of the charge as it leaves the muzzle; for on examining these wide-strewn pellets as they appear in a soft wood target or clay bank, I do not find them of a more uneven shape than most of those that reach the centre of the mark aimed at.

Now, though soft shot always becomes misshapen to a greater extent than hard, and the latter in consequence penetrates somewhat deeper, yet it does not kill better than the former, which penetrates sufficiently, and, from its superior weight, deals a heavier blow.

In regard to the choice of shot, hard or soft, I will write a few lines. *If*, as I maintain, the fact of shot becoming misshapen on its being fired has little, if any, effect upon its accurate flight, then, theoretically, I advise the use of soft shot, by reason of its being the heaviest; for across a strong wind its course is less affected than is the case with hard shot, as I have found by firing both kinds in a good breeze at a target 50 yards distant. The course of the hard, or lighter shot, is then deviated, as can be seen by the way its pattern is pulled off to right or left of the centre aimed at, according to the direction of the wind; whilst the flight of a charge of soft shot is not affected to a similar extent. At the same time, writing from *experience* in the field, I cannot, as they are *now* made, discover the slightest difference between soft and hard shot in their power of killing game up to 40 yards; so that if a young shooter chances to be using the one kind, he need not imagine he would kill better with the other.

THE GLANCING OF SHOT

I have often heard it argued whether shot will glance off game. I can answer this in the affirmative. The question of the glancing of shot first attracted my attention when watching a friend shooting at some duck flying low over a lake on a perfectly calm day. I noticed that, after each bird was struck, pellets seemed to drop in the water right and left, at an interval, after the charge had passed forward and the bird was killed.

It was a mere chance, and from my being favourably placed for observation, that I remarked these stray pellets fall. However, I determined to know more about it, so on the first opportunity I tested the question by suspending a dead pheasant on a string a couple of yards in front of a 10-ft. square sheet-iron target. I then fired several shots at the bird whilst swinging on its string—result, pellets diverged to the right and left in the form of splashes, showing, from their position well outside the ordinary circle of the shot-pattern, they were ricochets. Some of the pellets even struck my flanking targets *almost at right angles to the bird!* This proved—at all events to my satisfaction—that shot might easily glance off the smooth plumage of a bird in rapid motion with sufficient force, and at an angle acute enough, to explain some of the unaccountable accidents we hear of in field and covert.

What shooter, particularly in the case of driven grouse and partridges, has not frequently heard his shot rattle against the bird on its being struck, almost like peas thrown against a window! Depend upon it, this rattling is caused by the shot meeting hard substances, such as the quills of the wing-feathers, and perhaps the skull, bill, and legs, and is, to my mind, an evidence of glancing shot, the result very often of bone or quill in rapid motion being struck at an angle. Why, firing at a driven grouse flying down wind towards the shooter, is almost like firing at a stone, so far as the liability of some of the shot to glance off the hard and close-laid plumage of the bird is concerned!

ON SPECIAL LOADS FOR LONG SHOTS

For long shots (I do not mean *very* long shots—there is no use giving directions concerning *them*, as they are but chances) we must be able to put several pellets into the game. Accurate aiming is of no use if the pattern of a gun is so open at a long range that the game can fly through it without being struck. For long shots, from 45 to 50 yards for instance, 1⅛ oz. of No. 5 gives a much too scattered pattern when fired from a cylinder-gun; whilst the same measure of No. 6 gives us a pattern from which a bird would be far less likely to escape.

A shooter should bear in mind that to kill long shots he need *never* increase his powder *and* shot; he should either increase his powder, if using a cylinder, or, in the case of a choke, without altering his powder, reduce his shot. If his gun is properly bored, he can do this without its pattern suffering much. In both cases, however, an increased velocity is obtained, and that means additional penetration at a long range, if the game be struck—which, through loss of pattern to some extent, is not then so easy of achievement.

Increasing the powder is in some guns more likely to scatter the pattern than reducing the shot and leaving the powder alone; and if velocity is gained at a decided loss of pattern, there will, of course, be *no* advantage to the shooter in respect to long shots.

This loss of pattern is caused by the increased proportion of powder driving the shot at such a high rate of speed that a larger percentage of the charge than usual whirls off at a tangent on leaving the muzzle, instead of travelling up to the game, as it should do, in an even cluster, without a fringe of diverging pellets—which latter are, of course, wasted from being wide of the mark aimed at.

But if the shooter, by reducing his load of shot, can do away with these scattering and useless pellets, and *still* send up to the 30 in. circle as many, or very nearly as many, pellets as he did before making a change, and with a considerably higher velocity, he will *then* kill his game well at long distances. But he will have to *prove* this on his *target before* experimenting on *game*. He may take it for granted that the velocity of his shot is increased by reducing its bulk. The only thing for him to satisfy himself on is, whether his gun still makes a useful pattern on the target.

$3\frac{3}{16}$ dr. of powder and 1 oz. of No. 6 shot in a medium-choked 12-bore gun will kill game, if the aim be true, at unusual distances, and without undue recoil—always provided the gun is able to retain a regular spread with this charge.

$3\frac{1}{4}$ dr. of powder and 1 oz. of No. 5 would not answer in a cylinder, or even in a medium-choked gun, on account of the considerably less number of pellets this size of shot contains than does 1 oz. of No. 6; but in the hands of a first-rate shot, armed with a *full*-choke, some wonderful feats of shooting may be made with this load.

A very effective charge to use from a medium or full-choked 12-bore, $6\frac{3}{4}$ lb. gun, for long shots—and it were worth while to load for them—is 3¼ dr. of powder and 1⅜ oz. of No. 4 shot. A heavy shot like No. 4 has great striking force, and travels very fast to the mark, and with it the shooter need not, therefore, aim forward at long ranges to the same extent as when using No. 6. 1⅜ oz. of No. 4 contains but twenty-four less pellets than 1 oz. of No. 5, and gives a similar pattern, but is, of course, much superior to the latter in killing at long ranges. The larger the shot the less the recoil, and 1⅜ oz. of No. 4 will not be felt by the shooter more than 1⅛ oz. of No. 6; and though the above charge might be rather a smashing one for game, yet for occasional shots at hard-plumaged birds, such as wildfowl, it is well suited.

Few guns can, however, shoot No. 4 satisfactorily, so as to give a serviceable pattern, without being specially bored for the purpose, and then they may not perform so well as they ought with a usual size.

I have known shooters carry a couple of dozen or more cartridges, in a separate pocket or bag, especially loaded with an extra amount of powder *and* shot for very high birds, when they were aware of some spot during the day's sport where such were likely to occur. This is an error, as overloading a gun invariably means a weak and irregular pattern, when by leaving the powder alone, and merely reducing the amount of shot, or else increasing the powder only, the high or wild birds would be more likely to come down. Some of the tallest pheasants I ever saw killed were stopped with ⅞ oz. of No. 4, fired from a full-choked gun, the charge of powder being 3¼ dr.

It will be understood from what I have written that, when using a *medium* or *full*-choked gun, a shooter can afford to reduce his load of shot, and in this way gain superior penetration, without any increase of recoil, or noticeable loss of pattern *inside* the 30 in. circle. On the other hand, in regard to a *cylinder*-gun, he cannot spare *any* of the pellets in its charge, as the pattern of the 'cylinder' is more widely distributed than is that of the 'choke' at a long range; so that in the case of the cylinder we are forced to *add* to the powder without decreasing the shot, and to endure a slight increase of recoil to attain a superior velocity, and at the same time retain a good proportion of the usual pattern.

RECOIL

I have heard a few old-fashioned shooters, and especially keepers, remark that they like to feel a gun give a good kick on firing—their idea being that such is a proof the gun shoots hard.

This is quite wrong, as, with proper loading, undue recoil implies that the gun is a bad fit, and, for this reason, cannot be correctly held by the shooter when aiming; it then jumps in his grasp, and an erratic aim is a natural consequence. If a gun is too heavily charged, especially in the matter of shot, excessive recoil will, of course, result; and an overcharged gun will *never* shoot hard, though it may kick most unpleasantly. Small-bore guns recoil more in proportion than 12-bores, for various reasons; one being that they are, as a rule, overloaded with shot, with a view to obtaining *a good pattern*, which, if they *do* possess, it is *always at a loss of penetration*. If a 20-bore, for example, has the penetration of a No. 12, its pattern is much inferior. On the other hand, if its pattern resembles that of a No. 12, its penetration is inferior. A gun *must* be of a suitable weight in order to absorb the recoil of the charge of shot, if the latter is driven out with force to kill well, and at the same time contains enough pellets to make a useful pattern. It is in their efforts to attain these qualities in very light guns that the makers of the latter fail so signally; for they attempt an impossibility, and excessive recoil is the usual result!

LETTER XVIII

A FEW SIMPLE DIRECTIONS IN TARGET EXPERIMENTS, SUCH AS MAY BE OF USE IN TESTING THE EXCELLENCE, OR THE REVERSE, OF A GUN'S SHOOTING.

TARGET practice is of great service to a shooter, as by its means he can soon learn how a gun performs, and hence what may be expected of it in the field. Target experiments are the foundation of all *real* knowledge of a gun's game-shooting qualities, and without their aid we should be quite in the dark thereon.

A gun may be considered exceptionally good, but this reputation may merely result from the owner holding it straight. Often have I heard it remarked of a very ordinary shooting-gun that it was a wonderful killer, for shooters are fond of praising a gun to which they have taken a fancy, either from personal use, or from remarking how its owner—probably a good shot—drops his birds. All praise, or even blame, that a gun receives consequent on its performances at game is, in nine cases out of ten, bestowed for some reason having nothing to do with the actual shooting of the gun; *that* depends upon a variety of circumstances that are usually not taken into consideration by the critic a-field.

Perhaps the most ludicrous example I can give of the sort of way in which the shooting of a gun is sometimes judged occurred to me when killing some low-flying partridges in a turnip-field. A keeper, supposed to be above his fellows in his knowledge of guns and their merits, remarked, with a wise wag of his head, after I had fired several such shots:

' Sir, your gun shoots very hard. I can always tell a hard-shooting gun by the way in which the pellets *rattle on the leaves of the turnips!* '

Now, at a target a good or a bad shot can with equal confidence test the powers of a gun, and put out of the question all the many chances that occur for and against him when trying his gun on game.

ON LOADING FOR EXPERIMENTS

In all target experiments the cartridges should be carefully loaded—if possible, by yourself. It is not of such consequence that you should load the powder, if your gunmaker vouches for the correctness of the charge; but you should certainly count the number of pellets in every charge of shot. If your gunmaker can be depended upon, let him send you a hundred or so best cases loaded with powder only and properly wadded. Test two or three of the cartridges, to see they are correct, and fill them with shot as required for use.

Now, as it would take you all day to count the pellets of each charge of shot, should you fire even a moderate number, and as all shot measures are more or less inaccurate, and depend very much on how they are filled, you should purchase a shot counter, by using which all chance of a mistake from putting too many or too few pellets into a cartridge is avoided.

A shot counter can be regulated to one pellet, so as to hold exactly $1\frac{1}{8}$ oz. of No. 6 shot, or any other load desired; and it can be obtained for a small sum from a gunmaker.

To use the shot counter, all you have to do is to plunge it into a basin full of shot, rattle the pellets about till each hole has found an occupant, and then pour the surplus shot into the basin, and put the counted charge through a funnel into the cartridge. By this means every load of shot fired at the target is precisely similar. Without such being the case, experiments regarding the pattern of a gun, or comparisons taken between guns, are inaccurate, and, of course, unreliable.

The powder-charge, though not so important as far as a few grains go, one way or the other, still requires careful measurement in order to attain the exact quantity.

When measuring powder, the best plan is to take a

strong, new, empty cartridge-case, put a soft wad down on its base, inside, and over the latter a hard, thin wad. Carefully *weigh* in small glass scales just the powder-charge required, place it in the case, and shake it down with a few raps against the table. Next measure, with a piece of round wood that just fits inside the case, the height of the powder, and cut the case through level at that point, and you have a sufficiently accurate gauge for your powder; and several similar measures, marked outside with white paint, can be kept for various loads.

When testing a 12-bore, the charge of shot should be 1⅛ oz. of No. 6—that is, 304 pellets, being 270 pellets to one ounce. The charge of powder is optional, but usually consists in a 12-bore of 3 dr. or 3⅛ dr. of black, or 42 gr. of a nitro-compound.

Rightly enough, there is no exact definition for the powder-charge, as what we wish to obtain is the best pattern and penetration we can with the shot, and we have to discover a charge of powder that will do this. Some guns shoot well with less powder than others, and some with more; and whatever charge of powder the gun performs best with without undue recoil, *that* is the charge for the sportsman to use; for, so long as we confine the number of the shot-pellets when experimenting with one gun against another, the trial will be a perfectly fair one, for a gun falls off in its shooting when loaded with an *excess* of powder just as much as if loaded with too *little*.

PATTERNS OF GUNS

To commence, I will first allude to the pattern of a gun. It seems scarcely necessary, but I had better explain, that the pattern of a gun is the spread of the shot on the target—which pattern is good or bad according to the number of shot-marks the target contains, and the manner in which they are placed, whether regularly or the reverse. The regulation size of target at which guns are tried and compared for pattern is a circle of sheet-iron the diameter of which is 30 in., the regulation distance being 40 yards from the shooter's feet to the target.

The pattern a 12-bore cylinder-gun should put on a 30 in. circle at 40 yards will average about 130 pellets—a score shots being fired, each barrel alternately.

A bad-shooting cylinder-gun will place but 110 to 115 on the circle; a really good cylinder, from 130 to 135. I have had cylinder-guns that put an average of 135 pellets on the 30 in. circle, but these were exceptional weapons, and immense care had been expended on the boring of their barrels to cause them to behave so well. A gun that will regularly put 140 is never a pure cylinder, but is, at all events, one that throws the very *best* pattern for *all-round* shooting.

A medium-choked gun should place 150 to 160 pellets on a 30 in. circle, and a full-choked gun, 190 to 210, or even more. I have had guns that would make a pattern of 220 to 230; but by reason of the close patch of shot they threw up to the target, and the irregular way in which it flew—first to the right, and next to the left—I found it a very uncertain feat to kill birds on the wing at ordinary game-shooting distances. Clean misses occurred too often to please me, and birds riddled like a sieve or made rag-pie of when they *were* hit, did not please my friends when shooting with them, or myself when sporting at home. These *very* close-shooting guns are nonsensical for game-shooters to use, unless the latter desire to make the killing of what they aim at as *difficult* as possible; though, perhaps, if such guns were invariably fired at sitting game, they would be useful, as with care, combined with the aim of a rifleman, and, maybe, the advantage of resting the barrels on the top rail of a gate, the close patch of shot they throw might be put on the mark sighted.

A No. 16 cylinder should place from 115 to 120 pellets on the 30 in. circle at 40 yards, with 1 oz. of No. 6 shot and $2\frac{3}{4}$ dr. of powder.

The same gun, medium-choke, 140 to 145 pellets; full-choke, 170 to 180 pellets.

A No. 20 cylinder should place 95 to 100 pellets, with $\frac{7}{8}$ oz. of No. 6 shot and $2\frac{1}{4}$ dr. of powder.

A No. 20 medium-choke, 130 to 135 pellets; full-choke, 160 to 170 pellets, on the 30 in. circle.

It is worth notice here, that many small-bore guns, when put on their trial, are loaded with a *coarse powder*, such as No. 6, in order to obtain a good pattern, which they will then make, at *a loss of penetration*.

When a shooter orders a new gun, and requires it to make a particular pattern to his fancy, he should stipulate that it is to be tested with No. 4 black powder, or a nitro-compound (the former for preference), and No. 6 shot, of 270 *pellets to the ounce*. The latter condition he should not fail to enforce, or his gun may be credited with a fictitious pattern from the use in its trial of a size of shot containing more than 270 pellets to the ounce.

Even supposing the above guns make the required pattern of so many pellets on the 30 in. circle at 40 yards, there is still a good deal to notice in regard to their even spread of the charge of shot on the target, and also in regard to their accurate shooting to the centre of the target.

EVEN SPREAD

This implies that the shots fired cover the 30 in. target with a regular pattern and at equal distances one from the other, though a little closer together in the centre, as shown in Fig. 1. Therefore, the more accurate the aim of the sportsman the more pellets will be put into his game, and the cleaner will he kill it, especially as these centre pellets always strike the hardest.

If a cylinder-gun places its shot on the 30 in. circle in the form of a regular pattern at 40 yards, and 130 pellets can be counted therein, a partridge on the wing could not well escape being killed, or, at all events, being so disabled that it could easily be recovered.

A mistake often made by theorists is, that they

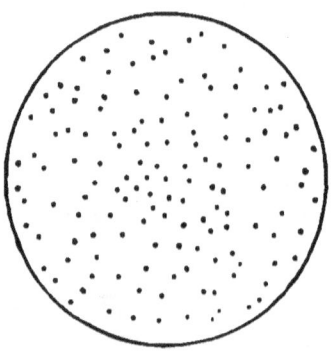

FIG. 1.—A GOOD PATTERN.

point to the pattern of a cylinder-gun on a target at the 40 yards (*a long shot*), and say :—

'Look! A partridge could escape being hit in this opening in the pattern of the shot!'

Now and then this might be the case, if the mark in question was always a bird sitting with closed wings; but in the case of a flying bird it may represent an object 18 in. wide, and one that is probably running the gauntlet of half the shot shown on the target as it passes across the diameter of the shot-circle.

IRREGULAR SPREAD

This is when the pattern is patchy, and shows open spaces on one part of the target and thick clusters on other parts, as represented in Fig. 2.

Through the open spaces the bird might escape; though the close patches, *if* they chanced to strike the mark, would kill well. But it were far better if the

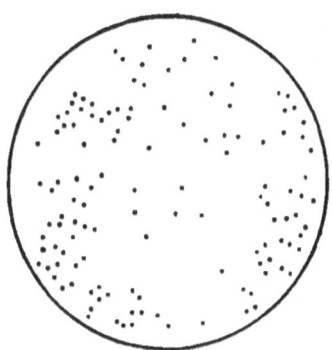

FIG. 2.—A BAD PATTERN.

grouped pellets were spread regularly over the target, so that there might be no open spaces, and then, whatever part of the shot-circle struck the game, it would kill it; for, of course, these close patches—the result of an irregularly shooting gun—vary with every shot, and cannot be depended upon to cover the object aimed at.

Fig. 3 is another example of a pattern that not rarely occurs in a carelessly bored gun, especially in a choke-bore. In this case we see a close patch of shot in the centre of the target, and the remainder of the charge so scattered as to be useless. The shooter who uses a gun that throws a pattern like Fig. 3 will now and then make very long shots, from by chance striking his mark with the thick group of pellets; but it is mere good luck his doing so, as the

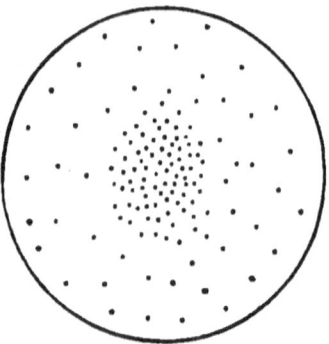

FIG. 3.—ANOTHER BAD PATTERN.

thick cluster of shot shown is liable to vary in its position with every shot fired, and he would kill with far more average certainty if the pellets were evenly distributed, as in Fig. 1.

THE ACCURACY OF A GUN

This is very important, and the want of it is most noticeable in a bad shooting gun, as, even should its pattern in the matter of 'even spread' and number of pellets it places within a *selected*[1] 30 in. circle be all that can be desired, yet the accuracy of the gun

[1] A *selected* pattern is one that is taken from *any* **part of a square 4 ft. target** by drawing a 30 in. circle round the closest group of shot, and ignoring whether this group appears on the proper 30 in. circle on the centre of the 4 ft. target, or if it appears in one corner of the latter; for this reason a *selected* pattern is *never to be trusted*.

may be quite at fault, and a very uncertain one to kill with as a result.

If a gun is *proved* to shoot true to the centre, then a target of 30 in. diameter is all that is needed to test its shooting; but as guns not unfrequently shoot aside of the mark, it is well to use a target on which there is space for any deflection to be easily detected. For this purpose the target (see Fig. 4) should be 4 ft. square, of thin sheet-iron, and secured with its centre level with the eye when the shooter puts the gun to his shoulder to aim. The cross-lines divide the target into equal parts, so that if a gun sends the bulk of the charge high or low, or to one side or the other, the fault can at once be perceived, and recorded for reference—'High right'—'High left,' or 'Low right' or 'Low left,' as the case may be. The circles and cross-lines should be cut into the metal as narrow as possible, and yet deep enough to give plain outlines.

The bullseye may consist of a bolt driven through the target, its head projecting half an inch—then it can be readily coated with black as required; it is impossible to aim a gun correctly at *any* target without a *distinct* centre at which to direct the sight. The rest of the target can be brushed over with whitewash after every shot.

When counting the pellet marks, learn to erase and count two at a time (either with the finger or the open end of an empty cartridge-case), and the pattern can then be quickly told up.

232   LETTERS TO YOUNG SHOOTERS   LETTER

When testing your gun for accuracy, aim, and fire, as with a rifle, at the bullseye on the 4 ft. square

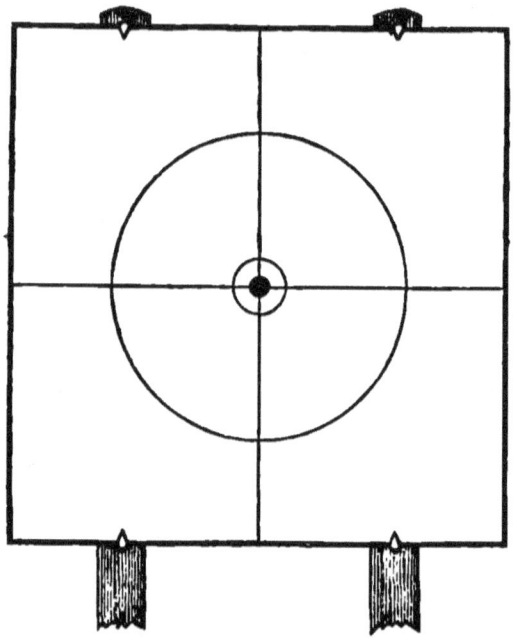

FIG. 4.—TARGET FOR TESTING THE PATTERN OF GAME-GUNS.
(Material, ⅛ sheet-iron, 4 feet square; large circle, 30 in. diameter; small circle 5 in. diameter; bullseye, 1¼ in. diameter. Cost, 1*l*.

target, choosing a time when there is no wind to influence the shot.[1] If the bulk of the charge is

---

[1] It is not so easy a feat as might be fancied to aim with *accuracy* time after time at a target with a game-gun, and practice will be necessary before a young shooter can do so successfully. Some shooters will do a gun full justice at a target, while others will not bring out its good points. For instance, shooting to one side or other of the target depends considerably on the shooter giving to the recoil, or the reverse; in the former case it causes the charge to shoot to the right, in the latter to the left. The pull of the triggers will also affect the aim, if these do not suit the finger of the shooter.

regularly placed *within* the circle, and you are conscious your aim was steady, then your gun is correct in the matter of shooting straight to a point.

If, on the other hand, the bulk of the shot is placed to one side, or high or low, time after time, *then*, if you can answer for your aim, the gun shoots inaccurately.

Should the bulk of the shot appear on the target on alternate sides, sometimes high, and sometimes low, it is probable your *aim* is more to blame than the *shooting* of the *gun*; for a gun that shoots inaccurately will repeat its fault in one direction.

The small, inner circle, of 5 inches in diameter, that surrounds the bullseye, should always contain (if the spread of the shot is satisfactory, and your gun shoots to the centre) some six or seven pellets, even if the barrels are cylinders.

A gun should shoot fair on the bullseye at 40 yards, and require no elevation, as all guns are arranged to shoot with a point-blank aim up to this distance; and, as a gun requires very little elevation of the muzzle to enable it to do so, shots at a less distance are not affected, especially as the pattern of shot is a good width, and allows a latitude of some inches one way or the other without causing a miss, as would occur in the case of a bullet from a rifle.

Many gunmakers give their guns the necessary elevation by raising the false breech like a step or back-sight above the barrels—an unsightly method. The best plan is to have barrels that taper from their breech-ends finely down to the muzzle; the shooter will then, on aiming, give sufficient elevation to his gun without other aids. Though one often hears it said that at long shots an elevation of the muzzle over the mark is required, I do not believe such is practically necessary when the width of the shot-circle at a long range is considered.

Measure your distance very carefully from the target, so as to ensure a correct 40 yards from its centre to the mark against which you put your toes when firing the gun; and if you wish to make *accurate* experiments, a 'rest,' covered at the top with soft cloth, will be required, on which to lay the barrels of the gun when aiming. So much for the pattern of a gun and how to find it.

THE PENETRATION OF A GUN

The next thing is a gun's penetration. This is not nearly so easy to discover, though there are many complicated appliances intended for the purpose. I will merely allude to simple methods, such as any shooter can apply for testing his gun, or to form a comparison between it and other guns, should he wish to do so. There is no doubt that the gun which gives an even spread of shot on the 30 in. circle is usually a good killer at ordinary ranges merely because, its load of shot being regularly scattered, the game cannot escape being struck should the aim be true. This fact is often the cause of a gun being alluded to as a hard hitter, though its penetration may be nothing out of the common.

A hard-hitting gun is one that drives its charge of shot up to the game in a compact mass, the pellets travelling from muzzle to mark with but a small proportion of their number straggling behind through a want of velocity, or diverging to the right and left.

A first-class shooting-gun and a weak one may both make *good patterns*, though one may shoot hard and the other just the contrary: as with the former the bulk of the pellets may reach the mark at the same instant; with the latter they may straggle up many feet behind the foremost ones—in which case the shooter has, perchance, not much more than half the amount of his load of shot at his disposal for killing a *crossing* bird, the remainder of the charge passing behind its tail.[1]

At a target this fault might not be discovered, as the pellets of the charge would probably all, or nearly

[1] It sometimes happens when four or five birds flying one after the other in line cross a shooter's aim, that he kills the *last*, though he *fired* at the *first*. The shooter at once concludes that he did not aim nearly far enough in front of the leading bird—in fact, that he ought, from the effect of his shot, to have fired as far forward of the first bird as the space that divided the first from the last. This reasoning is often very incorrect, as, though the *bulk* of the charge may have missed the first bird, it does not follow it struck the last—which latter may have been hit by a few chance pellets that straggled up after the real killing portion of the load of shot had passed on, possibly even in front of the original mark aimed at! As this is a

all, strike it, and the pattern might be excellent, for the slow pellets that would pass behind crossing *game* would reach the *target*, and be counted in the pattern.

The pellets that travel up to the mark slower than the rest of the charge are, of course, always the weak ones; and for this reason, when shooting at paper to find out penetration, it should be noticed if a number of shot stick in the first few sheets, as this is a sure sign the gun does not send its charge up in a concentrated form.

For the above reason, fire a gun at the 30 in. circle, and observe if a larger proportion of the pellets strike *below* the bullseye, instead of being spread regularly over the circle, as, if such is the case, it is also a sign of weakness in the shooting of a gun, proved by the dropping of the shot.

It is wonderful how the ear can be trained to detect how a gun throws its shot up to the target—whether loosely, in a stream of pellets, or in a compact mass.

Stand level with the target, a few yards to one

somewhat tough and technical letter (the fault rather of the subject than of my pen), I will enliven it by relating a remark once made by a keeper to a shooter on the latter complaining he so often shot behind his birds. ' Sir,' quoth the keeper, ' if your birds only flew *tail first* you would hit them all in the *head* ! ' Again, a gentleman once remarked of a neighbour whom he had invited to assist in shooting his coverts, and who was ' tailing ' all his birds, that he thought his friend would almost shoot behind the ' sea serpent '; when the head-keeper replied confidentially, ' he know'd nothing about no sea sarpents, but Mr. —— would certainly shoot behind a heel a-crossing a pond ! '

side, behind a safe shelter (well clear of walls or houses, so as to avoid reverberation), and cause a gun to be fired at the mark. After a little practice you can plainly discern whether the charge strikes in a 'bunch' with a 'smack,' or whether it rattles up in the form of a string of shot.

A 12-bore gun, with 1⅛ oz. of No. 6 shot (304 pellets) and 3⅛ dr. of powder, should penetrate, at 40 yards, with 5 or 6 pellets, 24 to 25 sheets of Pettitt's paper pads.

A 16-bore gun, 21 to 22 sheets, with 2¾ dr. powder and 1 oz. No 6 shot.

A 20-bore gun, 22 to 23 sheets, with 2¼ dr. powder and ⅞ oz. No 6 shot.

In these penetrations I refer to Pettitt's pads in their unseparated form.

Small-bore guns cannot avoid being inferior to a No. 12, either in pattern or penetration. Do as you may, you will not obtain a good pattern (one equalling a 12-bore) *and* a good penetration from them; either the one or the other quality will suffer.

If the charge of powder and shot is proportioned to the size of the bore, *then* 16-, 20-, and 28-bore guns should give about as much penetration as a 12-bore;

but they are *generally*—almost *always*, I may say—overloaded with shot to obtain a fair pattern, and naturally their penetration is weakened. Reduce the weight of shot in a small-bore below its usual bulk, and it will shoot as hard as a No. 12, but will then possess a killing-circle of small use save for close shots. Many of the so-called 28-bores are loaded with 1 oz. of No. 6 to 22 grains of a nitro-compound; this proportion is similar to the use of 28 grains of nitro, or 2 drams of black powder, with $1\frac{1}{4}$ oz. of shot in a No. 12—a charge from which no one could anticipate a fair amount of penetration!

The loads given above allow as much pattern as possible to the small bores; add more shot, and their penetration diminishes rapidly. We *must*, however, fire a pattern that will more or less cover the mark, so it is better to have one that will strike the game than one that is not likely to do so, from being too thin, though the force of the latter may be very high.

Messrs. T. Pettitt & Co., of 22 Frith Street, Soho, London, W., are the makers of the paper pads for testing penetration that bear their name. Each pad consists of 45 sheets of $9\frac{1}{2}$ in. by $10\frac{1}{2}$ in. brown paper, pressed together, and secured at their corners from coming apart, unless so desired by the shooter when he examines the sheets to see how many his shot has penetrated. These pads are apt to vary in toughness and substance, though for general experiment in regard to testing the power of a gun they are very useful. For *accurate* testing, as well as convenience in use, they should, however, be separated at the time of firing by means of a rack, as then, not only can the shot-holes be more readily recorded, but when each sheet of paper stands by itself a far more regular resistance is offered to the shot, and a more reliable record of the penetration of a gun is obtained in consequence.

I give on the next page a sketch of a simple and trustworthy arrangement I have used for testing the penetration of game-guns with the aid of sheets taken from Pettitt's pads. It consists of a sheet of copper rolled into a $9\frac{1}{2}$ in. in diameter tube, with divisions in the form of slits sawn down it at intervals of $\frac{3}{4}$ of an inch. The total length is about 3 ft.

> Fig. 1. shows the sheets of paper in position, excepting in the six slits at the end of the tube.
>
> Fig. 2. is the (or either) end of the tube, showing positions of sheets of paper in the slits.
>
> Fig. 3. Side view of a portion of the front end of the tube, with one sheet of paper only in position.

A A are the ends of an iron rod that runs all along the bottom of the tube, inside, to strengthen it, which ends are nailed down to a plank placed 4 ft. above ground on a trestle.

The tube should be placed exactly opposite the

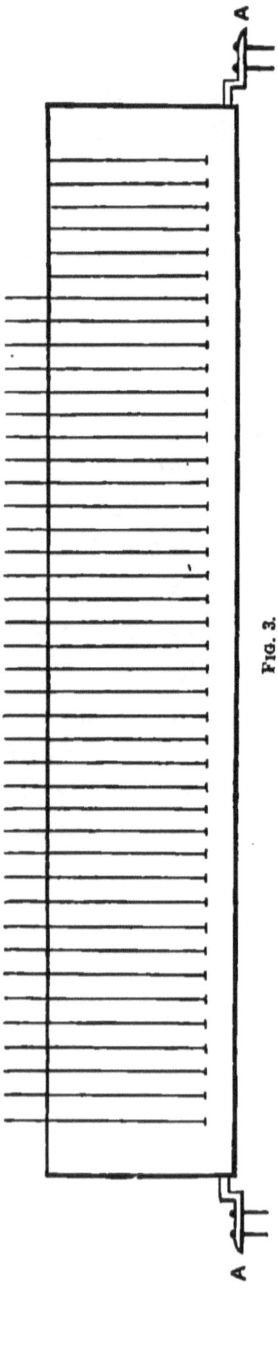

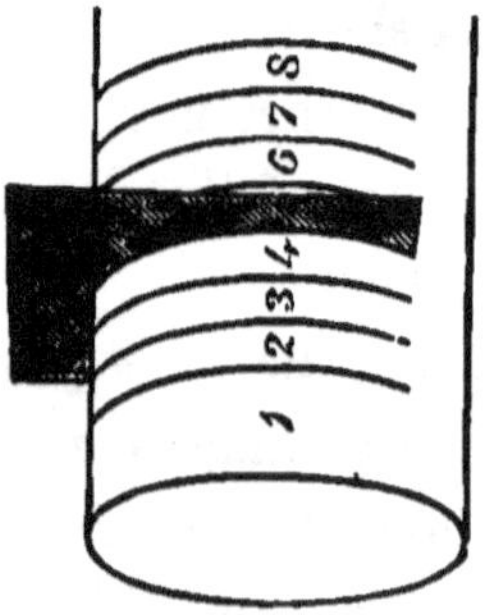

Fig. 1.

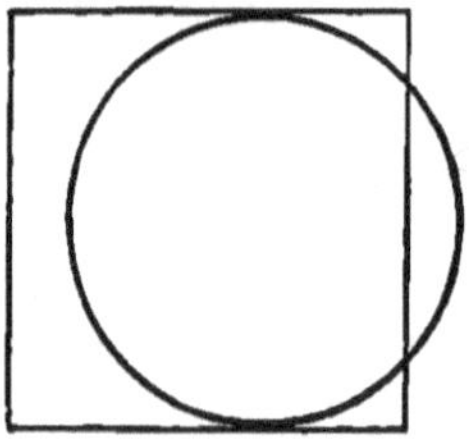

Fig. 2.

Fig. 3.

gun, and, with the aid of the numbers between the
slits, the shooter can on inspection at once see how
many sheets of paper his gun has penetrated. He
can also easily replace or move the sheets when they
are much perforated by the shot.

If a shooter is suspicious, after carrying out
experiments such as I have described, that a gun
does not shoot as hard or regularly as it ought (perhaps because he has not loaded it with a suitable
charge), let him act as follows, and load his gun, if a
12-bore, with $1\frac{1}{8}$ oz. of No. 6 shot, and, bearing in
mind the patterns various guns ought to make, as
before given, and taking into consideration what
pattern his gun should attain, according to whether
it is a cylinder or a choke, fire this load of shot at the
30 in. circle at 40 yards with $2\frac{1}{2}$ drs. of powder. The
shooter should notice the pattern as it improves in
even spread, and the number of pellets it contains
according as he increases the charge of powder, which
he can do, $\frac{1}{16}$th of a dram at a time, till he finds the
pattern does not improve, but remains the same, or
till it deteriorates. The pattern made by a 12-bore
will rarely be a good one if more than $3\frac{3}{16}$ drs. of
black powder or 45 gr. of chemical be used; and this
is a load that will generally cause more recoil than is
pleasant with most guns.

If the lower half of the target is more thickly
covered with pellets than the upper, though their

total number is sufficient, the charge of powder is too light. On the other hand, if the pellets are spluttered outside the 30 in. circle, and a too scattered pattern is shown inside, it is certain evidence that more powder is being used than necessary to the good shooting of the gun. A shooter who wishes to know what his gun will do in the matter of pattern *and* penetration, and is desirous of using a charge that suits it, should try various loads to this end. It is both useful and interesting to ascertain how a gun will perform with 1 oz. of shot. I have had 12-bore guns, cylinders even, that shot better, both as to penetration and pattern, with 1 oz. than they did with $1\frac{1}{8}$ oz.

Guns all vary, and if a shooter is not satisfied a gun shoots as well as it should do, experiments at the target are most useful; for, depend upon it, a man, however good a shot, will kill his game far better with a gun properly loaded than the reverse. Few people credit the difference in the shooting of a gun caused by the addition or subtraction of but $\frac{1}{16}$th of a dram of powder, or $\frac{1}{16}$th of an ounce of shot; and when we deal with an eighth instead of a sixteenth, it may just make all the difference in a gun's capabilities, and have a great effect on its performances in the hands of its owner in the field.[1]

[1] For years the Author has fired the same loads in his $6\frac{3}{4}$ lb. 12-bore game-guns (medium choke, pattern both barrels 150), namely, $1\frac{1}{16}$ oz. Newcastle No. 6 (270 pellets = 1 oz.) and $43\frac{1}{2}$ gr. Schultze Powder.

LETTER XIX

CARTRIDGES—CARTRIDGE-MAGAZINE—CART-RIDGE-BAG — SLEEVELETS FOR CART-RIDGE-CARRIERS OUT SHOOTING—GAME-BAG

I HAVE given young shooters such a dose of guns and precepts, powder and shot, that I really feel bound in the last two letters of this series to bestow a little amusement combined with instruction. With this intent I publish an 'olla podrida' of odds and ends connected with shooting, chiefly on subjects I am constantly receiving inquiries about.

CARTRIDGES

These should certainly be bought—excepting, of course, the few that may be loaded for the sake of experiment. It does not pay a shooter to fill his own cartridges, as he can procure them, not only considerably *cheaper*, but more *accurately loaded*, from a good gunmaker.

I advise the shooter to purchase the best cases, as they are but slightly more expensive than the worst, and do full justice to a gun—which cannot be said of their cheaper rivals. Kynoch's grouse-cases, covered with thin brass, are the pleasantest to shoot with I ever used, as wet cannot induce them to swell or stick. For wildfowl-shooters they are simply *invaluable*; and I always carry them, when afloat with the swivel gun, for killing wounded duck on the tidal flats, the cartridges being often loose in my pocket, and the latter generally saturated with *mud* and *salt water!*

The brown-paper cases, though they are a little less per hundred than the best blue or green, are much inferior in manufacture. They are not unfrequently of inaccurate gauge, especially in regard to their rims; they are also of weaker construction than the blue or green, and for this reason the base of a brown case will sometimes pull clean off when the extractor is used. If they get wet they soon swell, and then become at once unserviceable. They are very susceptible to damp, from the paper they are made of being soft; nor do they retain the powder with which they are loaded free from atmospheric influences, as I have realised to my cost when using some of these brown cases in wildfowl-shooting quarters where they have not been kept quite dry; though under the same conditions I have found the blue and green, and especially Kynoch's brass-covered cases, do not suffer.

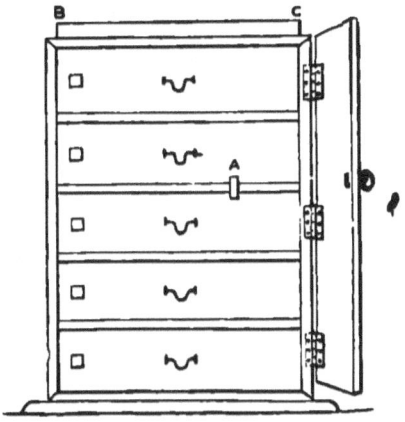

CARTRIDGE-MAGAZINE. Scale, ⅛ in. = 1 in.

To store 500 12-bore cartridges, placed upright on their bases.

Size of drawers, inside, 9¼ × 9¼ in. × 2½ in. deep.

The door, 3 in. wide, hinges flat to the drawers, and secures them all by the one lock at A.

The small tablets of bone or ivory (the size of visiting-cards) let in on the left side of the drawers are for recording in pencil the contents of the latter, when received, particulars of loads, and so forth. The top of the magazine has a rim (B C) all round its edge, 1½ in. high, of ½-in. wood, so as to form a hollow space in which to lay safely a few cartridges, cleaning materials, parts of gun-locks, screwdrivers, and such articles.

A magazine to store a larger number of cartridges can be constructed similar to the above, but with more drawers to it.

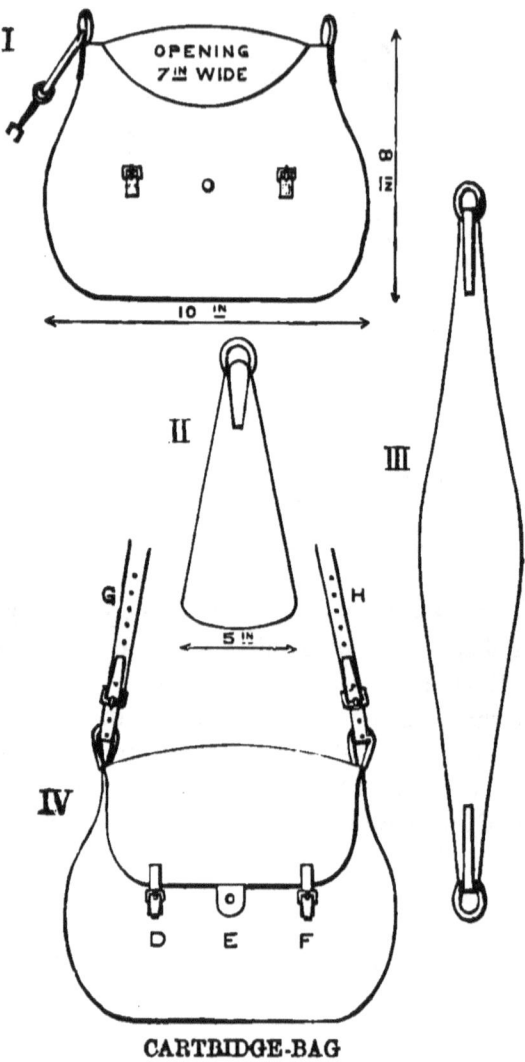

CARTRIDGE-BAG

For carrying cartridges in the field, nothing is so suitable as a bag made of strong yellow harness-leather, for it will last many years, and much longer than a bag made of canvas. The leather, if rubbed now and then with a waterproof mixture, will keep out all rain or damp. The best shape I give opposite. It should not cost more than about 12s. if made from this sketch by a *country* saddler; be sure it is made large enough. The weight of the bag itself is a trifle, and it is convenient to use one that will, if required, carry an extra number of cartridges, or that can be pressed for other services as well.

Fig. I. Cartridge-bag (without its flap), to take 80 cases.
Fig. II. Bag as seen sideways.
Fig. III. Bottom and sides of bag in *one piece*, the ends turned through brass rings and securely stitched.
Fig. IV. Bag complete. D F are small straps and buckles for fastening the bag when travelling, or in a game-cart. E is a large, loose-fitting stud and tongue to secure the flap down, as occasions demand, when the bag is in use. Opposite E, on the *reverse* side of the bag, at its back, there should be a *duplicate stud*, so that the flap can be turned back and buttoned out of the way when cartridges are required in a hurry, as at a 'hot corner,' or a 'busy' grouse-drive. The long shoulder-strap, G H, to be made of canvas web or leather, the latter for preference; it should be at least 3 in. broad over the shoulder, though narrowed at the ends.

Do not omit to have on your bag an extractor dangling by a small strap. See Fig. I.

The shoulder-strap has a buckle at each end; it is then detachable, and may at times be most useful, on an emergency, for securing a dog, broken harness, or for other purposes.

The corners of the bag, as shown in Fig. I., on each side of the 7-in. opening, are closed with separate leather pieces; and care should be taken that there is no crevice for rain to drip into the bag at these points when extended by its contents.

SLEEVELET FOR MEN CARRYING CARTRIDGES OUT SHOOTING

When a day's sport is arranged for several guns, each shooter on starting should be handed a number on a card, and a corresponding number (on a sleevelet) should be secured by a pin to the arm of the beater or keeper who carries his spare cartridges.[1] Then all

---

[1] Any reserve box of ammunition the shooter is likely to require the contents of, should also have his number on it in the form of a

that the shooter need do, when he requires his pockets or small bag refilled, is to call out his number, and the man who has the duplicate of it will at once bring him his cartridges, and a great deal of confusion and delay may be avoided. The sleevelet can be made of white calico or duck, with its numeral cut out of black cloth and sewn thereon.

When spare cartridges are carried indiscriminately by the beaters, it is not likely the latter can remember, even if they ever learnt them, the names of the various guns. For this reason, when out shooting we sometimes hear such a conversation as this: 'Bring Mr. Brown's cartridges, quick!' 'Which be Mr. Brown?' 'Why, the short, stout gemman.' 'There be two short gemman, keeper; which be he?' 'Why, dang thee, thou stupid, hurry up; yon's 'im, he as 'as no 'air on his 'ead.' 'I beant stupid; but 'ow can I tell what 'air is on his 'ead when 'ee's got his 'at on?' Now, if every gun and his cartridge-carrier have duplicate numbers in their possession, all this delay is saved, and perhaps a good deal of strong language on the part of Mr. Brown, particularly if the game is bolting past him and his uncharged gun, or if No. 16's are brought when his barrels are No. 12's.

As to keeping cartridges dry in a pocket during

label, so that a messenger may have no difficulty in finding it at once when despatched for the purpose.

rain, a hint may be useful. A shooter should always carry a light, rolled-up mackintosh;[1] he, of course, dons his spare coat in rain, and is then sure to find a difficulty in quickly taking his cartridges out of the pocket of his jacket when the latter is covered by his waterproof. To remedy this, he should have a slit cut in the latter, just *over* the pocket of his shooting-jacket, only *larger*, and fitted with a falling flap cover; he can then easily put his hand through to reach his cartridges from his inside coat, and he will keep them dry at the same time by means of the flap over the opening through the outer coat.

---

[1] The mackintosh coat is best carried in a small, square, waterproof bag that is closed by two buttons, with a strap for slinging over the shoulders; then no unstrapping or unrolling is required when its contents are demanded at short notice, and the coat is also protected from wet or unnecessary wear and tear. I know of only *one* style of mackintosh outfit for wet weather that enables a shooter to not only *shoot* with freedom, but to *walk* with comfort as well. This is a short coat without sleeves, reaching to the hips only, with a cape attached to it that can be turned back, so as to leave the arms free for aiming, and the right-hand corner of which can be *buttoned* back *behind* the *neck*, out of the way of the right arm. In connection with the coat, a kilt-shaped all-round apron reaching to the *knees*, and which buckles round the waist by means of a strap running round its upper edge. The kilt is, of course, open all down one side (secured with a button from flapping when windy), or else it would have to be stepped into or pulled overhead like a 'petticoat'—which would never do. A rig-out like this *looks* like a long coat, and keeps out the rain just as well (better in regard to the legs), but is a very different affair to *walk* and *shoot* in, as it has good ventilation, and none of the unpleasant drag or cling about the knees and waist that pertain to the ordinary shape. The coat to have *no* pockets, but large slits covered by flaps as above described. Messrs. Cording, 19 Piccadilly, may be consulted with advantage by any shooter who requires this outfit.

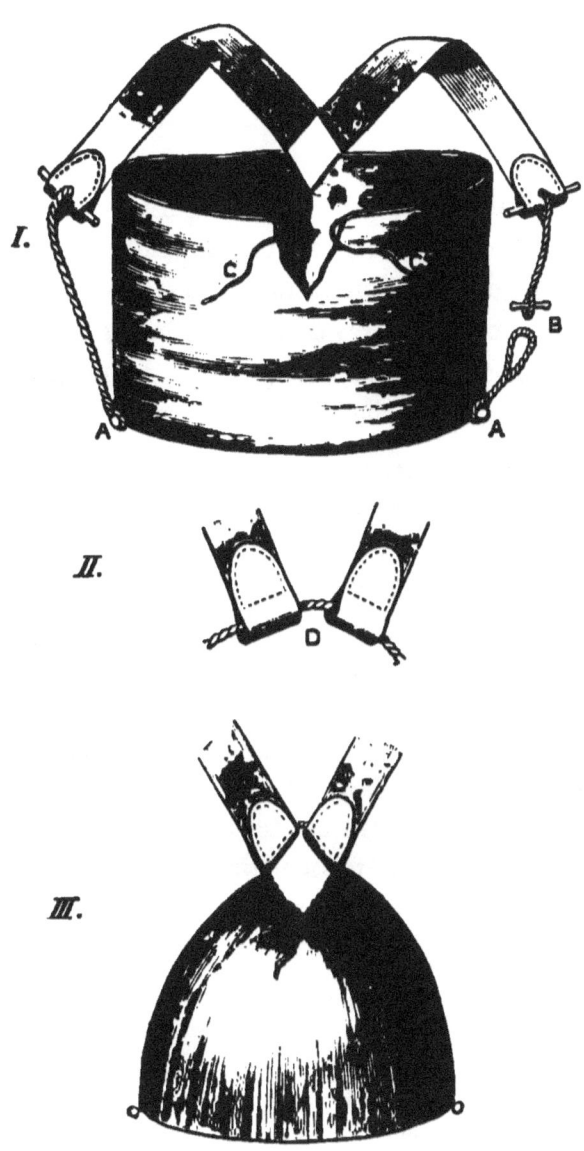

GAME-BAG

GAME-BAG

This knapsack game-bag (see previous page) is far easier and lighter to carry than the ordinary one, that hangs (and slips about) over one shoulder. It will not move from its position (unless the shooter stands on his head), and will carry a good number of birds. For a tramp alone it is admirable, as it does not in the least interfere with the use of the gun.[1]

Fig. I. shows bag open.

A A are small corks sewn into the corners of the bag to form knobs, and round which the cords are secured (rings are liable to tear off).

B is a detachable fastening in one cord (the right-hand one), so that the bag can be at once put on, or removed from, the shoulder.

C C are the ends of the strong cord (nearly as thick as a lead pencil) that runs *inside* the top edge of the bag and through the ends of the canvas straps, as shown at D, Fig. II.; which latter are strengthened with leather.

Fig. III., game-bag full, and closed for the road home, the ends of the cord being knotted up tight according to its contents.

---

[1] There is nothing new under the sun, and I am told, since I first penned the description of this capital game-bag, that it is an adaptation of the 'Rücksack' used by the chamois hunters of the 'Pyrenees.' I apologise to the chamois hunters for my unintentional piracy of their ideas!

Size of bag when open, 2 ft. wide by 18 in. deep; straps, 3 in. wide by 18 in. long; cords, 9 in. long. Material, light canvas.

GAME-BAG IN USE

LETTER XX

GAME-STOP — HOW TO MAKE RABBITS LIE OUT, AND HOW TO CATCH WOOD-PIGEONS

I HERE give a sketch of a contrivance for stopping game, on a covert being beaten, from breaking away into the open at the points and corners, as well as

GAME-STOP

for keeping the game inside a wood till the guns have taken up their positions—in fact, for general use as a 'stop' for covert-shooting. Size, 15½ in. long × 4¾ in.

broad × ¾ in. thick; length of swinging handle, 5¾ in.; nail-heads apart, centre to centre, 4½ in.; diameter of nail-heads, ¾ in.

The usual method of 'arming' a boy as a stop is to give him two sticks, with directions to beat them one against the other as he patrols certain weak points on the outside of a wood where the birds are likely to escape by the exercise of their legs.

Our boy generally 'whacks' his sticks together vigorously till masters and keepers are out of sight; he then turns his thoughts to other matters: tries if his pocket-knife is sharp; if, by peering round the corner, he can see the shooters; counts his marbles or halfpence—in fact, becomes terribly bored; though for fear of punishment he is as busy as a bee on the shooters coming in sight again, and then marches and whacks like a man—a return of energy that is sadly too late to be of service, for the pheasants probably stole away during his interim of idleness.

Now, to keep the boy up to his duty as a successful stop, the only method is to interest him in his act of making a noise; for I take it if he could play a fiddle, bang off a pistol, or beat a drum, he would never 'stop stopping'!

The game-stop I give a sketch of is well adapted for the purpose, and I will engage it will fascinate any ordinary village-boy for at least an hour at a stretch! By holding the stop downwards in his right hand, and twisting it from side to side, the boy can produce a gentle rap, rap, rap, or else the rat-a-tat-tat of a postman's knock—a noise quite sufficient to turn back into shelter an old cock pheasant that, with peering eyes and lowered head peeps through a hedge-bottom with the intent of a spurt 'over the fields and far away.' A piece of wood with a heavy box handle attached to it, the latter working easily from side to side in its fastenings, and striking alternately two big nail-heads, is all that it consists of; and it is similar to what is used for driving or stopping game at the grand battues of Austria and Germany. This stop can be easily made at home, or else obtained from any gunmaker, at a small cost, and is not only indestructible, but too simple to get out of order.

HOW TO MAKE RABBITS LIE OUT FOR SHOOTING

I wonder how often I hear this question asked? I will endeavour to answer it. There is not much difficulty in persuading rabbits to *leave* their holes by means of ferrets, or sulphur, paraffin, and other nasty smells. The job is to keep them from returning to ground again if *wet sets in*. In my experience, can they do so, *nothing* will prevent them from going home if *heavy rain* occurs; and we then, perhaps, see the disappointing (to a host at least) sight of six or seven friends, fully armed and thirsting for blood, setting forth to shoot 500 rabbits, and returning with 100 or less!

Placing paper on sticks at the mouths of the burrows, and other devices, are all very well in *dry* weather; but if we have *wet* the night before we shoot, the rabbits will certainly be conspicuous by their absence. Now, what we want is rabbits to shoot, wet *or* dry weather, *if* we have incurred the trouble and expense necessary to bolt them with a view to sport; and, when the rain beats against the windows, not to feel 'Poor sport to-morrow, for these blessed rabbits will have gone to ground!' but 'The rabbits, at all events, will be out, for they *can't* get back to their holes.'

The drawing on page 285 will explain how to outwit rabbits. The plan consists in surrounding their burrows, or a small wood, or even part of a wood, or banks, as the case may be, with 3-ft. wire-netting supported by upright posts. Against the netting, inside, lean boards (the front of a pheasant-coop is just the thing), and cover the upper surface of the boards with sods, so as to give them a natural look. Presently our little friends become hungry, and, after some hesitation, freely run up the ladders (so kindly placed) in order to escape from their wire fortress, and pop over one by one into their feeding-grounds outside. *Once outside, and there they have to stay*, for they cannot return home. The wire should either be sunk in the soil 6 in., or else bent outwards for 6 in. along the ground and pegged down, to hinder the animals from scratching underneath from the outside.

By properly surrounding the large burrows,

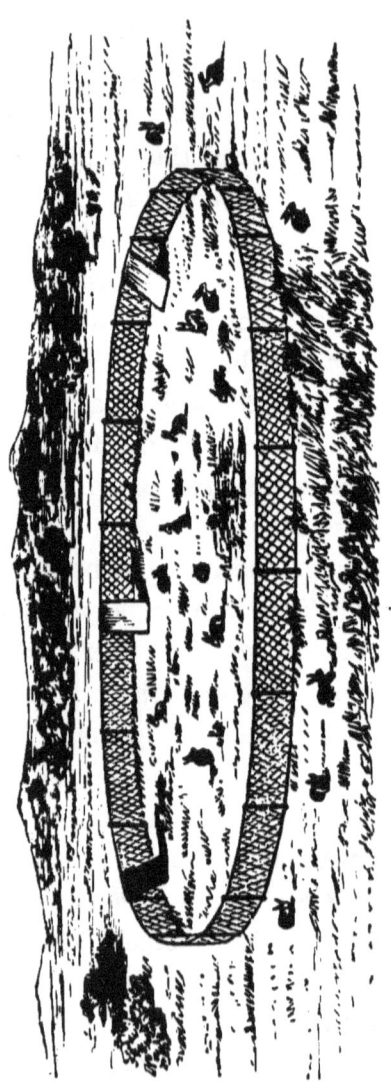

How to Make Rabbits Lie Out

whether in covert or open, as here described, every rabbit will come outside the wire that surrounds them in the course of three or four days in order to reach their usual feeding-ground, and all *should* find their way to the game-bag eventually, especially if there is some slight shelter for them to hide in not far off. Sprinkle a little dry soil or sand at the *top* of the turfed ladders, and you will soon see if the rabbits are coming out by noticing in the morning if they have beaten down the sand with their feet before 'taking off.' [1]

HOW TO CATCH WOOD-PIGEONS (*vide* next page)

'We have numbers, I may say thousands, of wood-pigeons every winter; but a few shots, and off they go, and we scarcely get a couple of score in the season.'

The above is a complaint I often hear. I will not now tell you how to *shoot* your wild pigeons, as that will eventually form a letter *by itself*, but I will give you a hint as to catching them, which may be of service to thin their numbers, especially as these birds are increasing rapidly, and, what is more, do considerable damage.

The cage (A) is merely formed of square 4-in. × 4-in.

[1] If you wish to *hurry* on your rabbit shoot, run a ferret with some oil of tar soaked into his coat (on the back), through the burrows a day previous to setting up the wire, which latter can be put down the following morning. By doing this a number of rabbits will be out to start with, which cannot return, and those inside will be hastened in their exit.

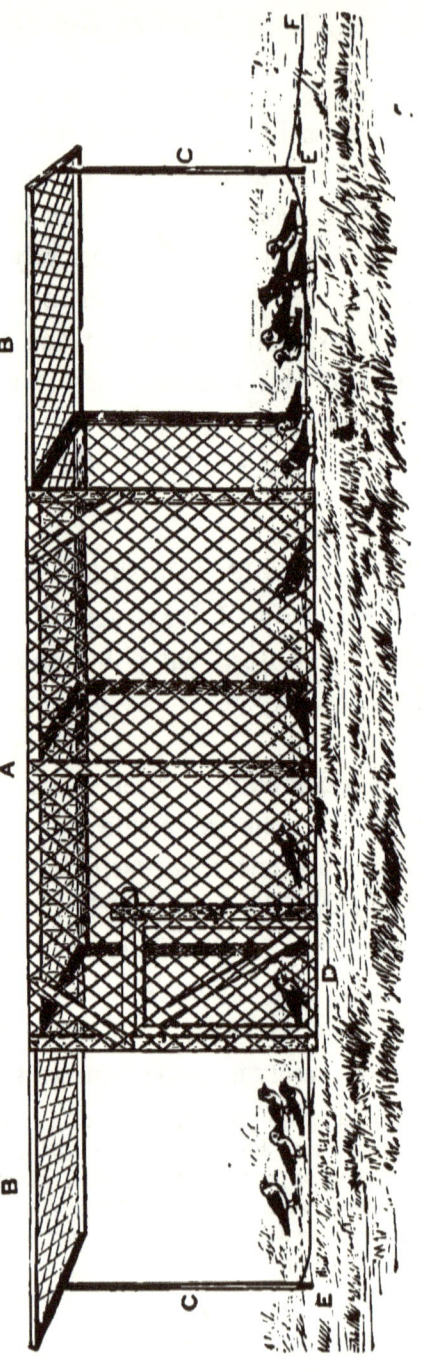

FIG 1.—WOOD-PIGEON CAGE.

posts driven into the ground and covered (except the ends) with 2-in. wire-netting. Size, 10 ft. long × 9 ft. wide × 5 ft. 6 in. high. At each end of the trap is a swing door, attached by hinges to the body of the cage, these doors, of course, being also covered with wire-netting.

The doors (B B), as seen in the sketch, are propped up by two long ¾-in. thick sticks (C C), and are so balanced ready for catching.

A galvanised wire, F (rats, rabbits, and wet would soon destroy string) is attached to the foot of the further stick, and runs along the ground, *through* the *inside* of the *cage*, to the next stick (see Fig. 1), and so on for 50 yards to the man in his shelter.

When the man in his shelter pulls the wire, he at once drags the lower ends of the long sticks simultaneously off their little posts placed level in the ground (E E, Fig. 1); the doors of the cage having then nothing to support them, down they come, and the pigeons inside are shut up from escape. As soon as the doors fall the man should rush from his concealment and, with two pieces of pointed stick, 1 ft. long, pin the doors tight against the cage so that no birds can creep out. He then enters the cage by means of the small door shown on its side (D), and kills and pockets the pigeons.

In Fig. 2, at E, it will be seen how the lower ends of the poles are lightly balanced on the small posts in the ground, with a penny or disc of brass (secured by a piece of wire) placed between them, to aid an easy slip off. The top of each stick is placed on the edge of the outer framework of its door, as in Fig. 1.

The best time for catching wood-pigeons is at daybreak, the man having hid himself in his shelter previously. The birds will then fly from the trees in which they have roosted down to the ground near the cage, and as they can see right through the latter when the doors are set up, will finally walk unsuspectingly inside in search of the corn that is ready

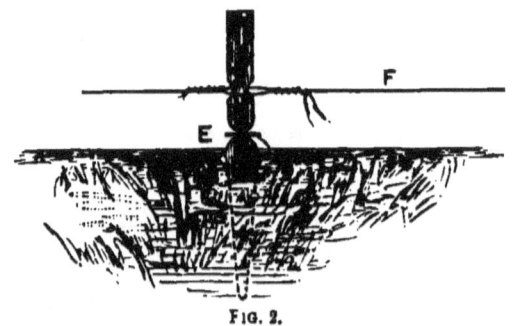

Fig. 2.

laid there.¹ In *hard* weather they will feed into the cage *any* time during the day. A catch should only be attempted every three or four days; the birds then *gradually* become fearless, and collect in numbers. They will walk about at first and pick up the corn scattered *outside* the cage; after a time they will finish this, and by degrees feed on the grain strewed *inside*. If only a few walk into the cage, do not catch

¹ Place some rakings and chaff down inside the cage and round it, so as to catch the attention of the birds as they fly overhead.

them, but leave these to act as decoys; they are sure to return, and will bring a larger number with them every visit. Thirty to fifty is a good catch if pigeons are about in large numbers.

The man will have to be well concealed, so that the birds that fly overhead cannot see him, or else they will sheer off and alarm the others. A roofed shelter made of tarred felt stretched over four posts, with a little window for inspection, and a seat handy, makes the best hiding-place. The pulling-wire can be led through a hole under the window. The shelter (placed among trees) can be covered with branches, to give it a similar appearance to the surroundings, or it can be made of fir-boughs entirely; but in the latter case it is, of course, not over-comfortable in wet and cold weather.

Place the cage in an opening in a wood near the trees in which the birds roost, as may be discovered by the droppings on the ground underneath.

A pigeon-cage answers admirably, as I have found from my own experience. I have known of as many as a thousand wood-pigeons being taken in *one* cage in a single season.

I now say 'Au revoir' to young shooters for a time, and in doing so I heartily wish them all 'Plenty to fire at, straight powder, kind friends, and good health.'

www.ingramcontent.com/pod-product-compliance
Lightning Source LLC
Chambersburg PA
CBHW031957230426
43672CB00010B/2188